Beyond the Hay Days

A Refreshingly Simple Guide To Effective
Horse Nutrition

REX A. EWING

Published by
PixyJack Press, LLC
LaSalle, Colorado

Dedication

To LaVonne Ann, who asked her cowboy to become a writer,
then gently nudged him away from his horses, and his hayfield,
long enough to become one.

BEYOND THE HAY DAYS

Published by PixyJack Press, LLC
P.O. Box 575, LaSalle, CO 80645 USA

First Edition 1997

Library of Congress Catalog Card Number: 97-68266
ISBN 0-9658098-0-3

Printed in the U.S.A.

Book designed by LaVonne Ewing.
Cover and interior illustrations by Sara Tuttle.

Contents

Prologue

The horse is a spirit that lies so deeply buried within the human psyche that we often do not even realize it is there. And yet it is everywhere; there is no end to our fascination with these incredibly canny beasts. Even after 100 years of forsaking the horse for the horseless carriage (motorized transportation), the horse is still imbedded in our language. "Get back on the horse!" or "Quit horsing around!" are still common admonitions. On a summer day you might drive to a picnic in a vehicle rated in horsepower, eat sandwiches seasoned with horseradish sauce, then swat a few horseflies while playing a game of horseshoes. Look through any magazine—even one tailored to computer buffs—and you will see pictures of gracefully striding horses. Watch television on any given night and you will see ghostly images of the mythical, winged horse, Pegasus, morphing into a sporty new car.

Those of us who keep horses can only smile. We live a dream embraced by those who wish horses into their lives, only to find that they do not appear. Many people sell their homes in the city and, at no small expense, move to the country, just to be able to have a piece of that dream; a horse or two to ride and show. Others, like myself, have lived with horses for so long, a month in the tidal pools of New Guinea could not hide the fact from the nose of the common observer. We talk horses, we think horses, and we smell like horses. And we're proud of it.

I have always had horses in my life. I have been kicked and bitten, stomped on, bucked-off, and slammed into more fences than I care to recall. I have hobbled out of the house on crutches to ask the horse who did it to me if he was ready for the next round. I'm sure you know what I mean. If all of this abuse had been heaped upon me by the federal government, I would be looking for another country. But a horse is not a thing you can walk away from, or destroy. It is much too big for that; too big in sheer mass to manhandle, too big in spirit to deny.

From August of 1990 until April of this year, I was the president and CEO of a well-known company that derives nearly all of its revenues from the manufacture and sale of nutritional supplements for horses. It was not a job that I had dreamed of having, and I never felt that it suited my sensibilities, but it did set me on a seven-year mission to learn, as much as any simple horseman can, the best ways to help our horses through nutrition.

This book is the result of that seven year search. In that time I have formulated a number of supplements that have been very successful in the marketplace, and equally successful for the horses in whose feed they ultimately ended up. But supplements are only the icing on the cake, not the cake itself. Most of the people who sought my advice over that time did not need supplements, at all. They needed good, sound, basic nutrition; they needed to know what was inherently wrong with their feeding program, and how to correct it.

And that is my reason for writing this book. It was a fundamental decision, like drinking to slake a thirst, or eating to fill an empty belly. I had to write it because I owed it to the thousands of horse owners I have met and corresponded with over the years who needed a book such as this. People who, like all of us, wanted only the best for the beasts who are the keepers of our dreams.

Rex A. Ewing
July, 1997

Acknowledgements

I wish, first and foremost, to thank my wife, LaVonne, for her help in making *Beyond the Hay Days* what it is. Her tactful encouragement during the darker times always reminded me that the distant light at the end of the long tunnel was not the headlight of an oncoming train, as it so often seemed, but a beacon to light the path to the book's completion. Usually it was she, holding the lantern. No one but LaVonne could have taken my bare-bones computer files—unorganized and untitled—and breathed life into them, quite the way she did.

There are very few mothers who would support (and subsidize) an education nearly so unstructured as mine, but my mother did, and since I drew from every aspect of my college education in writing *Beyond The Hay Days*, she deserves my thanks. She also decided, long ago, that I could heal from anything my horses could do to me, so she never discouraged me from keeping company with them.

My father, a gentleman, a horseman, and a self-proclaimed "dirty gut fighter", taught me that defiance, against ugly odds, is a virtue; that nutrition is a science, feeding is an art, and the proper combination of the two is a little luck, and a lot of intuition. He also instilled in me the wisdom that getting back in the saddle was the only honorable thing to do, even if the ground tended to get harder and farther way with each successive landing upon it.

Every reader will be grateful for the many fine illustrations by Sara Tuttle—who also did the paintings for the cover of the book—and I owe her my special thanks.

I would also like to thank Dr. Donald Mackey for reading my manuscript and making several insightful suggestions and corrections. Dr. Mackey has been in practice longer than I have been around to bang up horses for him to treat, and several generations of horses have led better lives for that fact. In addition to the knowledge about nutrition-related diseases that he has shared with me over the years, Dr. Mackey has taught me a number of techniques that have helped me to better care for my horses. My favorite was a graphically detailed, hands-on tutorial on how close not to stand to a horse when administering a tranquilizing dart.

Lou Reed, a good friend, a keeper of horses, and a woman of no small erudition, graciously agreed to take time away from her busy schedule to read my manuscript. Had she not, the readers of this book would have had to wade through a number of untenable grammatical permutations, inaccessible to anyone but me. Thanks, Lou.

I would also like to thank Dr. Earl E. Ammerman, friend and mentor, who knows more about minerals than most people know about their spouses; Dr. Larry Mackey, the only veterinarian I know of with a Master's degree in nutrition, who still gets all of my emergency calls, even if his left-handed techniques and my right-handed bungling does lead to an occasional wreck; Joe and Lee Hatch, who together produce the best horse feeds found anywhere, and who bring a refreshing degree of integrity to the feed industry; and Jim Olson, nutritionist, who took me under his wing when I was young and naïve, and answered more of my nutritional questions than most fathers have to answer of their children who are going through the terrible "why?" stage. *Beyond The Hay Days* has been greatly enriched by their suggestions and corrections.

Of course, any mistakes, omissions, understatements, overstatements, lapses of good judgment or grammatical snafus are entirely my own.

Introduction

THE ART
OF NUTRITION

J ust below our house, in the Platte River valley on the eastern slope of Colorado, my wife and I have about 15 acres of what is called sub-irrigated pasture. The water table is at, or just below, the surface. This is land that has never been farmed, and never will be. It is too wet for the plow, it is even too wet for most trees and broadleaf weeds. But it does produce an excellent variety of grass, that stays vibrantly green from late April through mid-October, and will easily support 15 horses during those months, even in a drought.

All of the minerals deposited there, through floods and other geologic forces over the millennia, are still there. The manure left by the horses today is washed back into the soil to be taken up into the new-growth grass again tomorrow. I have never had this grass analyzed, so from a scientific standpoint, I don't really know what is in it, and what isn't. But from a practical standpoint, I know that it will keep my horses healthy and happy for seven months of the year, as long as I deworm them regularly, and provide them with water and salt. I also know that if I give my horses extra feed, they will have shinier coats, healthier feet, and brighter eyes. My foals will grow bigger and stronger, and their mothers will produce more milk.

When I feed supplements and sweet feed, I know exactly what I am giving to my horses, right down to the last milligram. Many would think it strange, or even remiss, that I would feed supplements without knowing the composition of the greater part of my horses' diets. How could I introduce such a large unknown into a controlled feeding program?

But what, exactly, is unknown? I know that the grass they are eating provides nutrients within a range that is natural for the horse. If it didn't, I would see problems I have never seen in horses on this pasture. I also know that there is nothing toxic in the grass—it has never caused lameness, gastric distress, abortions, abnormal growth, or unusual behavior. I know, just like my father knew before I was born, that this particular 15 acres of ground provides almost everything a horse needs to live a long and healthy life, which is far more than I know about the things I feed myself!

There are hundreds of nutritionists that will analyze, to the last microgram, every nutrient in every speck of food a horse eats. I am not one of them. It is as pointless an endeavor as it is a boring one. The science of feeding horses is nothing like the science of building bridges. Every cable, every I-beam that comes out of a steel mill is built to a very narrow range of tolerances that can be plugged into an equation that will let the engineer know what stresses the bridge will be able to endure. Not so with horses. Just as no two horses take to the bit quite the same way, or feel exactly alike under saddle, no two horses share the same biological makeup, or nutritional tolerances. One horse will colic and die eating the same hay another horse can eat day after day without so much as a mild bellyache. An accidental grain ration sufficient to founder this horse will do nothing to that one.

And even if horses were as standardized as I-beams—a thoroughly depressing thought—the nutrients we give them are not. Fifty milligrams of copper looks the same on a guaranteed analysis, whether it is supplied by copper sulfate, or copper proteinate, or copper polysaccharide complex, but the amounts of copper ions making their way through the intestinal wall and into the blood stream are quite different with each one.

The issue at hand is as simple as it is profound: there is a point where the science of horse nutrition must graciously defer to the art of horse nutrition, and it is up to each horse owner to decide where that point is, with every horse he or she owns. My pasture of "unknown" content is, for me, the beginning of an art that began with the domestication of the horse. I could have it analyzed for mineral content, protein, and energy, but I would still not know what was in my pasture. Each blade of grass is endowed with hundreds, if not thousands, of nutrients, each more subtle and elusive than the one before it. Unanalyzed, undissected—it remains a whole, beyond quantification, beyond science.

Those of you reading this book, who truly love your horses, will understand immediately what I am talking about. There is a science of reining, and an art of reining. This is so with racing, jumping, and any of a hundred other disciplines. And so it is with nutrition.

It is the spirit of the horse that we love, not the veins and the hormones, and the bones. It is the spirit that draws us to them, again and again, no matter how large, no matter how costly, no matter how dangerous. There is something in the horse, far beyond our meager attempts at analyzing it, that we want for ourselves. And therein lies the core of the art of horsemanship.

By the time you finish reading this book, you will be able to read any feed label with the confidence of knowing when you are being buffaloed, and when you are not. You will be familiar with the major constituents of forages, feeds and supplements, and you will have a good idea of how much of each is good for your horse. There will be a lot of science in this book, because science is the language of units and degrees, and any treatise on horse nutrition would be lacking without them. But as you read this book, remember: no one knows your horse as you do, and no one ever will. You may think you bought him for his svelte body and his kind eye, but you really bought him because he was your horse; his spirit touched yours. If this book helps you, in some small way, to keep that spirit strong and willing, then it has done its job. And you will have learned quite a bit about the art of horse nutrition.

Chapter 1

FEEDING AS A FUNCTION OF DESIGN

F eeding a horse would, intuitively, seem to be a very simple proposition. After all, horses did quite well on their own for several million years before would-be, Bronze Age horsemen made the historic discovery that it made more sense to feed the horse and let it do the work, than to eat the horse and do the work themselves. In fact, a maintenance horse kept on a good pasture can do quite well with no more additions to the diet than water and salt. But most of us do not have the luxury of a good pasture; most horses are kept in stalls with small runs that provide no more in vegetation than the occasional weed to chew on.

By nature, horses are grazers, which means, simply, that their natural food of choice is grass. While this fact is evident, it does lead to a couple of conclusions that need to be considered. First, that the horse's natural diet has a very high moisture content and, second, that it is natural for the horse to eat small amounts of feed on a continual basis. If we contrast these facts with the common feeding practices of today—dry feed given in large amounts two times a day—we are left with a glaring disparity between what the horse is built for, and what it is offered. It is no small wonder the leading cause of mortality in horses is colic. The mystery is that most horses do as well as they do.

The horse's stomach is quite small compared to that of its bovine companion, the cow. The horse has a single stomach that can hold no more than two to three gallons of liquid, while a cow has a four-part stomach, the first part of which—the rumen—can hold up to 40 gallons. While cows digest most of their feed in the stomach (about 70%), the horse only digests 8% - 9% of its feed there. The bulk of the horse's digestive processes are completed in the small and large intestines. Most of the soluble nutrients are broken down by enzymes and absorbed in the small intestine, while the more insoluble material passes into the large intestine where it is worked on by enzymes produced by colonies of bacteria. This is why horses are referred to as "hindgut fermenters". The problem is, the large intestine is not of uniform diameter throughout; it contains several bottlenecks and tight, serpentine turns—great places for impaction to occur.

The horse's digestive system is designed to move a continuous stream of moist, fibrous material, and it is very important for us, as their keepers, to approximate those natural conditions as closely as possible. Anyone who has ever spent much time around a large herd of horses knows that they are quite adept at finding ways to block their bowels (sand, rubber fencing, wood chip bedding, etc.) without any help from us. We lost an excellent race horse to an impaction a few years ago. A postmortem examination revealed a large ball of cords from a rubber fence as the cause of the blockage. The horse was 4 years old, but he had not been in a pen with that type of fencing since he was a yearling; he had carried that time-bomb with him for three years.

Since most of us cannot pasture our horses year round, we have to make the best use of what we have to work with. The basis of any feeding program should be a good quality hay. Most hays (alfalfa and grass) contain around 30% fiber on a dry matter basis, much of it insoluble. And even though insoluble fiber provides little in the way of nutrition, it plays an essential role in the dynamics of the digestive system by absorbing water and assisting the flow of material through the gut. In other words, hay rehydrates in the gut, recreating, as closely as possible, the conditions the horse is anatomically suited to.

Unfortunately, most hay is not sufficiently nutrient-laden to supply a majority of horses with everything they need to be the shiny, healthy animals we so admire. There is simply not enough energy in most hay to meet a horse's enormous nutritional demands. To do that, we have to add concentrated, high-energy feed to the diet; things that are low in fiber. But as long as we do it wisely, and bear in mind the horse's digestive limitations, there should not be any problem.

_____ *Feeding as a Function of Design*

Part One

ENERGY:
THE NUTRIENTS THAT SUPPLY IT
AND THE HORSE'S NEEDS FOR IT

Chapter 2

ENERGY:
FUEL FOR THE EQUINE ENGINE

Energy is required by a horse for every single activity it engages in, from running a race, to digesting its food, to blinking its eyes. The energy requirements of a horse are often overlooked in favor of more exotic solutions to what might be a very simple problem. Horses low in energy lose weight and condition, and refuse to work. The growth of young horses is slowed. Mares come into heat later in the season, and can have prolonged gestation periods. And often all that is needed is better quality hay and a little more grain.

All of the energy used by the horse is derived from three classes of nutrients: carbohydrates, fats, and proteins. When the chemical bonds that hold these nutrients together are broken, energy is released and work is performed. The energy requirement of horses is expressed as Digestible Energy (DE), which is the energy in its feed minus the energy in its feces. DE is measured in Mcals (megacalories), each Mcal is equal to 1000 kcals (kilocalories), which is the standard measure of food energy for humans. (For the sake of simplicity, I have converted Mcals to kcals—or more commonly known just as calories—throughout the book.)

Just how much energy does a horse require? In chemistry, a calorie is the amount of heat required to raise the temperature of one gram of water one degree Celsius at normal atmospheric pressure.

This means that each calorie (kcal) we eat would increase the temperature of 1000 grams of water (one liter) by one degree Celsius, or would take 10 grams of water from freezing to boiling. An average working horse that eats 19.6 Mcals (19,600 calories) of digestible energy per day consumes enough energy to turn a 55 gallon drum of ice into a boiling cauldron, a fact that really ought to give you a new respect for hay and oats.

How is the food energy from hay and oats turned into energy to warm the body and keep muscles contracting? All living things, from blades of grass to horses, use the same universal compound to provide energy: ATP, or adenosine triphosphate. As the "tri" in triphosphate suggests, the molecule ends with three phosphate groups held tightly together by very high energy bonds. It is the energy in the final bond that is of particular importance; the energy in that one bond supplies all the energy a horse uses for everything, from chewing its food to running a grueling, head-to-head race.

ATP is continuously broken down and reassembled by two different modes of respiration to supply the body with needed energy. The quickest of the two, the anaerobic, works without oxygen, while the other, the aerobic, requires oxygen. Let's look at the merits and limitations of each, without making things too complicated.

ANAEROBIC RESPIRATION

Anaerobic respiration is performed in twelve steps. Steps one through ten, interestingly, are identical to the fermentation process used in making wine and beer. Sugar, such as glucose in the case of the horse, is broken down into two molecules of lactic acid (or ethanol, in the fermentation of wine and beer). Two molecules of ATP are used to produce four, for a net gain of two molecules of ATP.

Anaerobic respiration is not especially efficient, though it is fast. In an all-out quarter-mile sprint, almost all of the energy supplied to a horse's muscles is by this means. Since the burning of every gram of sugar produces two grams of lactic acid as waste, in a very short time the muscles are overcome with this lactic acid "exhaust", causing them to ache and burn, and become weak.

AEROBIC RESPIRATION

Aerobic respiration is far more efficient than anaerobic. One molecule of glucose will produce 36 molecules of ATP, with water and carbon dioxide as the only waste products. In addition, protein and fat can be used as fuel, as well as glucose. The only drawbacks of aerobic respiration are that it is slow and it requires oxygen, neither of which is usually a problem for most horses. A fit horse in a race of a mile or more will derive about half of its energy aerobically, an endurance horse on a 50-mile trek even more. And of course, standing in the pasture eating grass is entirely an aerobic activity.

Chapter 3

THE NUTRIENTS THAT SUPPLY ENERGY

CARBOHYDRATES

Carbohydrates are the primary source of energy for horses. They are the main constituents of hay and grain, making them the most conspicuous part of a horse's diet. All carbohydrates are composed of three elements: carbon, hydrogen and oxygen. As the word "hydrate" would suggest, the hydrogen and oxygen are in the same 2:1 ratio as water. Plants use sunlight in a photosynthetic process to combine atmospheric carbon dioxide and water into carbohydrates, and return the extra oxygen to the atmosphere, so horses and horsemen can keep on breathing and exhaling carbon dioxide, so plants can go on growing. It is a very nice exchange.

Glucose, or blood sugar, is also the sugar manufactured by plants during photosynthesis. It is a simple sugar with six carbon atoms attached to the equivalent of six molecules of water. When glucose is linked to itself in long chains it forms molecules of glycogen, a polysaccharide, which is to the horse what starch is to the potato: stored food. Glycogen is the primary fuel of the body. It is stored in the muscle cells, the liver, and in the fat around the liver, so for most short-term activities there is plenty of fuel around when it is needed.

The fiber that makes up such a large percentage of a horse's diet consists of several types of polysaccharides, all with varying degrees of digestibility. Soluble fiber is easily digested, while insoluble fiber, such as cellulose, is worked on by microflora in the gut, with marginal success.

FAT

Dietary fat is broken down in the body into fatty acids, which circulate through the blood and are stored throughout the body (especially between muscle cells). Like carbohydrates, fats are composed of atoms of carbon, hydrogen and oxygen, but the levels of carbon and hydrogen are much higher. This makes for stronger chemical bonds and more energy released when they are broken, making fat a high-energy nutrient. All fats are soluble in ether, but not water. If you read a feed table looking for "Crude Fat", it may not be there; if not, look for "Ether Extract"—same difference. Ounce for ounce, fat has 2.25 times more energy than carbohydrates or protein.

Although fat is a very small part of most equine diets (both today, and in the past when horses roamed the Great Plains), horses do possess a surprising ability to digest fat. Many trainers are taking advantage of that fact by adding fat to the diet of their horses in training. Since fat can only be burned aerobically, it is of questionable benefit for horses in an all-out performance, but can help horses during slower, paced activities. Because fat is such a concentrated feed, using fat to replace some of the grain in a performance horse's diet can help to achieve a comparable energy balance with less bulk. An ounce of corn oil contains about 255 calories of digestible energy. Corn oil is a very palatable fat for horses, and it can be added to the diet liberally, though there is a point at which a horse will refuse to eat it.

PROTEIN

The body can also burn protein as fuel, after the nitrogen has been removed and the carbon chain has broken down. But like fat, protein can only be burned aerobically, in the presence of oxygen. During a grueling performance, when glycogen stores in the muscles are nearly depleted, protein is pulled from nearby muscle cells and burned as fuel if there is no other source of energy available.

As an energy source, protein is not a wise choice. It contains no more energy than carbohydrates, and it is several times more expensive to feed. But there is a lot more to protein than its energy value. Protein's main role should not be as a fuel, but as a building material......

Protein: The Stuff Your Horse Is Made Of

If horses possessed the same abilities as the plants they eat, all we would have to do is feed them a little ammonium nitrate, some simple sugars, and a few trace minerals. With those ingredients they could make all the protein they would ever need, and we could dispense with this section of the book. But evolution is economical; if the plant can do it, the animal eating the plant shouldn't have to, so better use of limited biological resources can be made in other directions.

Actually, it is not protein the horse needs, but the amino acids that are the building blocks of protein. Horses make their own protein at the cellular level, if all the right amino acids are available. But while some amino acids are manufactured by bacteria in the hindgut, there are 11 amino acids that either cannot be synthesized, or cannot be synthesized in sufficient quantity, and must be fed to the horse. These are known as essential amino acids. There are about as many amino acids as there are letters in the alphabet (25, or thereabouts) and since proteins are really nothing but long chains of amino acids, there are as many possible proteins as there are combinations of letters, which is to say, for all intents and purposes, an endless number.

Proteins are in every cell in the body—they are the very basis of protoplasm. They provide the framework for the structure of the body. Proteins are absolutely necessary for the growth and maintenance of muscle tissue, enzymes, cartilage and connective tissue, blood cells, hooves, hair—you name it: if it's a functional part of the horse, then part of it is protein.

To maintain good health, a horse needs—depending on its stage of life and level of activity—between 8% and 15% protein in the total diet, figured on a dry matter basis. If there is not enough protein in the diet, the horse will develop a dry and lusterless haircoat, a loss of appetite, slow hoof growth and, if the condition goes unchecked, loss of body tissue.

There is a direct correlation between protein and energy: a horse will need between 40 to 50 grams of protein for each Mcal (1,000 calories) of digestible energy, with the maintenance horse on the low end, and the lactating mare on the high end of the spectrum.

While hay and pasture are the primary sources of protein for the horse, many (if not most) horses will require an additional protein source, depending on the quality of the forage. Good quality alfalfa hay cut in the early stages and put up right, can be as high as 20% protein soon after it is baled, with the protein content slowly dwindling during storage. On the other hand, bromegrass hay can be as little as 5% protein, or as high as 14%, depending on when it is cut, and how it is harvested. Timothy, Bermudagrass and orchardgrass usually contain somewhere between 7% and 13% protein. The earlier hay is cut, and the sooner it is baled, the better.

Cereal grains also contain varying levels of protein. Oats, depending on the grade, are between 9% and 14% protein, barley between 11% and 13%, and corn between 7.5% and 12%. Other sources of protein include soybean meal (45%), cottonseed meal

(41%), and linseed meal (35%).

All of these values are for crude protein, not digestible protein. Some proteins are of a higher quality than others. High quality proteins supply more of the amino acids the horse needs, and and of those proteins, some are more digestible than others. Alfalfa hay that is 18% crude protein, for instance, will be about 13% digestible protein, while a grass hay with 13% crude protein will only be about 7% digestible protein.

Is digestible protein important? Yes, but values for it are difficult to determine. Most feed manuals list protein concentrations of feed as crude protein. To be on the safe side, you should provide your horse with several protein sources. If you suspect that none of these sources is giving your horse the quality of protein it needs, supplementation with the amino acid, lysine, can greatly improve the total protein quality, as lysine appears to be the most critical of the essential amino acids.

Finally, since so many horsemen are also cattlemen, I should mention non-protein nitrogen sources, such as urea. These compounds are converted into protein, either by the horse itself, or by bacteria in the gut. Although urea has been shown to be of definite benefit to cattle, a horse's digestive machinery is not as adept at making protein as their bovine counterparts. By the same token, a horse's lack of ability to utilize urea gives it a higher tolerance to it, since much of it is excreted before it is converted into toxic levels of ammonia in the hindgut. But is it worth the trouble to feed it? No—the risk of accidental poisoning is too great, and far outweighs any benefit. But if you feed it anyway, there are two things to remember: urea should not be fed to mature horses at a rate of more than 4% of the total diet, and it is better not to feed it to young horses, at all, since they do not possess the same tolerance for it that older horses do.

Chapter 4

PUTTING THINGS INTO PERSPECTIVE WITH A BIGGER AND BETTER TROJAN HORSE

Everyone has heard of the Trojan War—the ten-year battle between the Greeks of Sparta and the Trojans of Troy (or Ilium). Legend has it that the war began following the abduction of the world's most beautiful woman, and ended after a clever deception, centered around the world's biggest horse. It was a giant steed, fashioned from wood and steel, by the battle-weary Greeks, and made hollow to hold the warriors that would sack and burn Troy, once the horse was pulled within the city's walls. Although Virgil, in his epic poem *The Aenid*, never gives the dimensions of the Trojan Horse, it is reputed to have held a thousand warriors. A sizable horse, by any standards. But in order to put into perspective the units of measure found on feed labels these days, I am going to propose an even bigger horse—one that is made of flesh and bone (of the imaginary variety). First we need to become familiar with some common feed industry terminology.

Anyone who has ever taken the time to read the guaranteed analysis on a feed tag, or a bucket of horse supplement, has probably noticed that all of the nutrients are listed in comparative units, such as "mg./lb." or "PPM". Specifically, you will find five such units of measure, if your feed label is printed according to AAFCO (Association of American Feed Control Officers) guidelines and regulations:

% (percent) Used to guarantee protein and amino acids, fat, fiber, and macrominerals, such as calcium, phosphorus, salt, and magnesium.

IU/lb. (International Units per Pound) Used only to guarantee the fat soluble vitamins A, E, and D.

PPM An acronym for "Parts per Million", also equal to milligrams per kilogram. Trace minerals, such as copper, cobalt, zinc, etc. should be guaranteed in PPM.

mg./lb. Milligrams per pound. Used primarily to guarantee the water soluble vitamins, such as thiamin, pyridoxine, niacin, etc. A milligram is $1/453,600^{th}$ of a pound.

mcg./lb. (or µg./lb.) Micrograms per pound. Sometimes used to express guarantees of minute amounts of certain nutrients such as vitamin B_{12}. A microgram is $1/453,600,000^{th}$ of a pound.

After years of formulating feed supplements and preparing the labels to go with them, it occurred to me that I had no concept of what a part-per-million or a milligram-per-pound was, in everyday, familiar terms. It is easy enough to do the math and learn that one particular unit is such and such a fraction of another, but to really comprehend the meaning of the numbers requires a leap of the imagination.

Since a mastery of these terms is necessary to fully understand the quantities of nutrients going into our horses, I thought it would be helpful to use the Trojan Horse analogy to bring these tiny but essential amounts into the human realm, by using things of everyday experience for comparison. I will not use percentages, since they speak for themselves, or IU/lb., because the amounts vary from vitamin to vitamin, but PPM, mg./lb., and mcg./lb. are ripe for illumination. Before we go on, it might be helpful to give a one-dimensional analogy: if a pound were 1000 miles, a gram would be 2.2 miles; a milligram 11 feet, 8 inches; and a microgram $1/8^{th}$ of an inch. Interesting, but it's even better in 3-D.

To start with, a pound is not the fourth part of a coffee can of grain anymore—it is a room in your house. Let's make this room 12' by 12', with an eight foot ceiling. It may be your bedroom, or perhaps your kitchen (with all of the furniture, cabinets, and appliances removed, please). Now, what could we put in this big, empty room to represent one PPM? A cherry tomato is just about right. Take this conceptual cherry tomato, set it in the corner, and be happy knowing that you are only 999,999 cherry tomatoes away from filling your kitchen with small, red, bullet-proof salad vegetables.

To represent one milligram (a thousandths of a gram) in our room-sized pound we can go a bit bigger: all the way up to a large egg. But if we want to demonstrate the size of one microgram (a millionth of a gram) we have to search around in the cabinets we just removed to find one, tiny peppercorn.

But remember, our room is just one pound, and a horse eats several pounds of feed every day. In fact, extending our analogy, each day our Trojan Horse eats the equivalent of a 2400 square foot house, full to the rafters with feed.

Just how big is this house-eating horse? From the ground to the withers, it is 192 feet (or, if you wish, 576 hands). From the tip of its nose to the base of its tail it is 328 feet, or a little longer than a football field. Its legs are over 110 feet long, and 14 feet in diameter at the knees. It could cover the 1¼ miles of the Kentucky Derby in about five strides.

If we feed this horse 15 milligrams of biotin per day to maintain its enormous hooves—they span 20 feet—the biotin would occupy the volume of a mere 15 chicken eggs.

And by the way, if we were to hollow this horse out and use it as a siege engine, it would hold somewhere in the neighborhood of 13,200 Greek warriors, or cowboys, depending on whether we were attacking Troy or Dallas.

Now that we have a clear understanding of the relative pro-portions of the units used throughout the book—as well as on all feed and supplement labels—we can examine the nutrients that are guaranteed in those units, and how they apply to different classes of horses.

Chapter 5

THE FUNDAMENTALS: ENERGY & PROTEIN REQUIREMENTS

Anyone who has ever paged through a horse magazine or a mailing from one of the larger catalog houses has no doubt come to the conclusion that it is possible to indulge a horse with an endless variety of feeds and supplements. Every day a new company will pop onto the scene, claiming that they, and they alone, have the solution to all of your horse's problems. It often reminds me of a modern-day version of the traveling medicine show, where tonics were proffered that cured everything from corns to consumption. But the fact is, if you can sort through the fantastic claims being made by a few unscrupulous manufacturers, there really are some very good products on the market that have proved beneficial to thousands of horses. We have learned a lot about nutrition in the past ten or twenty years, and the result has been a boon to horsemen who have been able to educate themselves enough to sort through the hoopla. Hopefully, after reading this book you will be able to decide what is good for your horse, and what is only good for the manufacturer's bottom line.

For now, though, we will only concern ourselves with the basics; energy and protein, and a few more of the essentials that are critically important to different classes of horses. In Part Two, as we go through the "Nutrients That Do Not Supply Energy", we will refer back to the horse classes discussed here to fill out the requirements.

Please note that the requirements listed for the various classes of horses are minimum amounts needed to maintain health.[1] They are not necessarily <u>optimum</u> amounts. Certain nutrients, such as calcium and phosphorus should be fed at rates close to the amounts listed, while others, like vitamin A, can and probably should be fed at higher levels. If this raises a cloud of confusion, it should dissipate during the discussion of the individual nutrients. The "Guide to Supplemental Feeding" (starting on page 105) should further clear the air.

MAINTENANCE HORSES

The maintenance horse is an animal that spends a blissfully boring life in the pasture, or in a small run behind the house. It spends its days standing in one spot, wondering when dinner will be served, or amuses itself by trying to stretch its neck far enough to reach a few blades of grass on the neighbor's side of the fence. He might be an old gelding that you ride a little on weekends, if you have the time, or a horse injured in competition that needs a little rest. An empty mare, or a mare just bred and without foal, fits the maintenance category, too. What do these horses need, nutritionally, to keep weight on and their coats shiny, to maintain the gleam in their eyes, and to give you a run for your money when you ride them too close to the fire-breathing Rottweiler your neighbor keeps chained up in his yard? This will be a good start:

1 A mature body weight of 1100 lbs. has been assumed for all horses in the following examples. The nutrient amounts may be adjusted for larger or smaller horses, bearing in mind that—as a general rule—smaller horses require a slightly higher level of nutrients per pound than larger horses.

Daily Needs of 1100 lb. Maintenance Horse
Based on Total Dry Feed Intake of 18 lbs. per day

Digestible Energy	16,400 Calories	Magnesium	8 g.
Crude Protein (10%)	655 g.	Zinc	327 mg.
Calcium	22 g.	Copper	82 mg.
Phosphorus	14 g.	Vitamin A	15,000 IU

Although this is only a few of the nutrients known to be necessary to the horse, it covers most of the major ones, so it will nicely serve our purpose here. Below is a comparison of two types of hay: sun-cured alfalfa in mid-bloom (this is about as good as hay gets), and sun-cured bromegrass, in the late stages of growth, a far more pedestrian type of hay. [2]

Comparison of Hay
Based on Total Dry Feed Intake of 18 lbs. per day

	Alfalfa	Bromegrass
Digestible Energy (Calories)	16,800	14,900
Crude Protein	1526 g.	490 g.
Calcium	111.0 g.	20.7 g.
Phosphorus	19.6 g.	18 g.
Magnesium	28.6 g.	9.8 g.
Zinc	253 mg.	196 mg.
Copper	144 mg.	82 mg.
Vitamin A	376,360 IU	90,000 IU

And who said that horse nutrition was a difficult subject? Just give that horse a couple of flakes of top-quality alfalfa hay morning and night, plenty of water and salt, and you're home free; nothing could be easier. With the exception of a few milligrams of

---

2 Most of the information in these feed analyses is adapted from the National Research Council's "Nutrient Requirements of Horses, Fifth Revised Edition, 1989", a must book for any serious student of horse nutrition.

zinc, the alfalfa hay has everything the horse needs to keep going. The calcium to phosphorus ratio in this hay is over 5 to 1, far too high for a growing foal, but marginally acceptable in a mature, maintenance horse. At any rate, the ratio could easily be brought into line by the addition of monosodium phosphate to the salt.

The bromegrass hay, on the other hand, falls a little short of the mark in digestible energy (calories) and far short in protein. To keep that airy little bounce in this horse's step, we need to find a way to get the protein level up and add a few more calories to its diet. Let's add one pound of soybean meal, and three pounds of oats:

Adjusted Ration
To Raise the Protein Level and Number of Calories

	Bromegrass Hay	Soybean Meal	Oats	Total
Dry Feed Intake (lbs.)	14	1	3	**18**
Digestible Energy (Calories)	10,780	1600	4350	**16,730**
Crude Protein (g.)	381	226	181	**788**
Calcium (g.)	16.5	1.8	1.2	**19.5**
Phosphorus (g.)	14	3.2	5.2	**22.4**
Magnesium (g.)	7.6	1.4	2.2	**11.2**
Zinc (mg.)	152	26	53	**231**
Copper (mg.)	66	10	9	**85**
Vitamin A (IU)	74,375	0	60	**74,435**

We are getting a little closer with this ration. Phosphorus is higher than calcium, but should be safe. We have the protein up to over 9%,[3] which is acceptable with a maintenance horse, and we have enough calories to meet its barest energy demands. Unfortunately, because protein is so expensive, we are now spending nearly as much money on the one pound of soybean meal as we are on the 16 pounds of hay, and they don't give oats away, either. If we add

3 See the Appendix, page 126, for the formula to calculate total protein in mixed rations.

The Fundamentals

just ½ pound of soybean meal and 5 pounds of oats, fed with 12½ pounds of hay, the protein is still around 9% and we have saved a little money. Of course, we are assuming that the bromegrass hay was put up under the right conditions and stored out of the weather, since rain and sunlight can leach the nutrients out of hay in short order. If this horse were stressed by bad teeth, parasites, bad weather, or disease, its nutritional needs would increase sharply. But we have solved a problem arising from poor quality hay, and offered a basic idea of the process of calculating a workable ration. These rations are only two of hundreds of possible rations, any one of which would work equally as well. (Note that zinc is low in every one of these rations and should be supplemented in some form.) Obviously the best solution would be to find better hay, but that is not always possible.

Our maintenance horse would most likely do quite well on one of the bromegrass, oats, and soybean meal diets. A lot of horses have done well on less. Of course, this horse is the easiest of all types of horses to keep; it is through growing, and it doesn't have to expend much energy to stay alive. As these factors come into play, the art of feeding becomes increasingly more interesting.

PERFORMANCE HORSES

These are the horses that capture the imaginations of everyone—horsemen and non-horsemen alike. They are the sleek competitors in the Triple Crown races, the muscular acrobats in Britain's Grand National, and the stocky speedsters in the All American Futurity. But they also include the marathon runners of the endurance races so popular in the American west, and the hard-working roping and barrel horses in American rodeos; they are the trotters and the walkers and the chariot racers. Everyday these horses try to win against the best of the best, and the nutrition they are provided is one-third of the winning equation, equal in importance to training and genetics.

Entire books have been written on the subject of feeding the performance horse, and it would be folly for me to try to condense even a fraction of that knowledge into a few short pages. There are as many nutritional formulas for winning competitions as there are nutritionists. But any feeding program that is worth its salt begins with energy. If the performance horse lacks energy, everything else is academic.

The energy requirements of a horse in heavy training are easily double those of a maintenance horse. While the dietary energy needed by a maintenance horse is around 16,400 calories per day, a horse at the track on a demanding racing schedule can easily burn up 32,000 calories daily or more. It would take over 45 pounds of the late-stage bromegrass hay we analyzed earlier to supply that much energy, or 36 pounds of high-grade alfalfa hay. Obviously, this is not acceptable, even if a horse could eat that much hay (and I have seen a few that could). A more concentrated source of energy is required, such as a mixture of corn and oats. While corn is a very high-energy feed, it is extremely low in fiber, which is also needed in the diet. It is a good policy to mix oats in at least a 1:1 ratio with corn. The following diet should safely supply the energy needs of an 1100 lb. race horse:

High Quality Alfalfa Hay (14 lbs., dry)	14,500 Calories
Corn (7 lbs., dry)	12,200 Calories
Oats (7 lbs., dry)	10,150 Calories
Total	**36,850 Calories**

But what about protein? If high-quality hay is fed—and by that I mean hay that is in the 18% - 19% range—the total ration will be around 14% - 15% protein, which will be plenty. Unfortunately, this type of hay is not easy to find. Hay in the 10% - 13% range is more the norm, which means an additional protein source may be required, such as soybean meal or cottonseed meal. Many feed mills carry fortified sweet feeds in the 12% - 16% range. The better feeds contain a liberal sprinkling of essential vitamins and minerals.

Daily Needs of 1100 lb. Performance Horse in Heavy Training
Based on Total Dry Feed Intake of 25.3 lbs. per day

Digestible Energy	32,700 Calories	Magnesium	15.1 g.
Crude Protein (11.4%)	1309 g.	Zinc	459 mg.
Calcium	40 g.	Copper	114.9 mg.
Phosphorus	28.5 g.	Vitamin A	22,453 IU

While it is a good practice to put as much hay in the diet as possible, many owners and trainers feed only 20% hay in the entire ration, making up the difference with oats, corn, barley, molasses, fat, soybean meal, and various mixtures of vitamins and minerals. Such a small amount of hay can be dangerous, and is not recommended, yet many horses do quite well on such a diet.

Just as the energy needs of a performance horse can be double those of a maintenance horse, the need for other nutrients increases too, but not necessarily on a one-to-one basis. The requirement for some nutrients, such as vitamin E, more than doubles, while others, like copper, increase by less than half. And even if the nutritional needs were simply an arithmetic progression, we cannot practically feed a performance horse twice the amount we feed a maintenance horse. A high-quality ration, sensibly fortified with vitamins and minerals is a must. Differences between individual horses that may appear slight under normal conditions, are often magnified when horses are stressed by heavy training schedules. Some horses lose weight, no matter what they are fed, others refuse to eat. Many of these problems are nutritionally related conditions peculiar to a certain horse, and most can be solved by the right feeding regimen.

A horse just coming out of competition and reduced to maintenance horse status should be let down slowly. This horse is sleek and muscular; its belly is tightly tucked up, and it is constantly on the move. It is as high as a kite. It likes its feed and it likes being fast and powerful. It is a mistake to make immediate and drastic changes in this horse's diet. The feed should be taken away slowly, over a period of weeks. Once the horse has calmed down and adjusted to its new life, it will need only maintenance levels of nutrition until the next training season.

There are several nutrients beyond those ordinarily found in hay and sweet feed that can be beneficial to performance horses. Each of these nutrients will be discussed at length in _Part Two: Nutrients That Don't Supply Energy_. You may also wish to refer to the supplementation table on pages 107 and 108.

STALLIONS

I have always found stallions to be the most fascinating of horses. In stallions, the human emotions of jealousy and possessiveness are laid bare, free of posturing and pretense. Stallions make it quite clear what they want, and what they are willing to do to get it. They are hell on fences and—should one happen to get loose—other horses. A stallion fight is a singular event of enormous power and fearsome savagery, in which the two combatants will fight until one or both lie prostrate on the ground, having not even the energy left to stand.

All of this hormone-driven passion carries a price tag. My Thoroughbred stallion needs twice the sweet feed my old gelding needs to maintain his weight, even in the fall, long after the end of breeding season. The stallion devours minerals the gelding turns his nose up at. Statistically, the stallion should not need all that extra feed. In fact, a stallion's estimated nutritional requirements are all only about 12% - 15% above a maintenance horse of the same weight.

The wild card with stallions is energy. The NRC estimates that an 1100 pound breeding stallion should have a minimum of 20,500 calories in the diet. Some high-strung stallions will wither away with that little energy, others will do quite well. It is important to keep a stallion in good condition, neither too fat nor too thin. Routine exercise can help keep the stallion in condition, and take his mind off the duties he so amorously pursues—for a time, anyway. Occasionally a stallion will develop the same problems some track horses do: excessive nervousness and loss of appetite. The addition of thiamin (vitamin B_1) to the feed can usually help such horses.

Daily Needs of 1100 lb. Breeding Stallion
Based on Total Dry Feed Intake of 18.8 lbs. per day

Digestible Energy	20,500 Calories	Magnesium	9.4 g.
Crude Protein (9.6%)	818 g.	Zinc	341 mg.
Calcium	25 g.	Copper	85.3 mg.
Phosphorus	17.8 g.	Vitamin A	22,453 IU

Keep a watchful eye on your stallion. Watch his feed, his performance, and his condition. He depends on you for his health and his livelihood, just as you depend on him for the results of his charged libido.

BROODMARES

Just like expectant human mothers, the nutritional needs of broodmares change over time. The difference is that they cannot run to the local convenience store at midnight to procure the nutrients they need in a bizarre collage of junk foods—they have to rely on you to feed them everything they need for their foals to be born healthy, and to stay that way. It is your responsibility to keep a watchful eye on your mare to be certain that she stays in condition—neither too fat nor too thin, with a healthy haircoat and plenty of energy.

The nutritional needs of a pregnant mare without a nursing foal at side are the same as for a maintenance horse for the first few months. But by the eighth or ninth month, her nutritional needs will rise sharply. The foal inside of her is growing at a geometric rate, and if she is not given enough of what she requires to sustain that growth, she will pull nutrients out of her own tissues and bones to ensure that growth will continue. At this point, minerals are of paramount importance. While her energy needs will increase by only 15% - 20%, her needs for calcium and phosphorus will nearly double. Following are some of the daily nutritional requirements for an 1100 pound mare in the third trimester of pregnancy.

Daily Needs of 1100 lb. Pregnant Mare (3rd Trimester)
Based on Total Dry Feed Intake of 18 lbs. per day

Digestible Energy	19,600 calories	Magnesium	9.4 g.
Crude Protein (10%)	864 g.	Zinc	327 mg.
Calcium	38 g.	Copper	82 mg.
Phosphorus	28 g.	Vitamin A	29,940 IU

Once the mare foals and begins producing 20 to 30 pounds of milk per day, she will need 40% - 50% more digestible energy, and 70% - 80% more calcium and phosphorus than she did before parturition. Although she will need more energy at this time, care should be taken during the first week to ten days after foaling not to give the mare so much grain that the foal develops milk scours.

Following are a mare's daily requirements for these same nutrients, after the foal is born:

| **Daily Needs of 1100 lb. Lactating Mare** | | | |
Based on Total Dry Feed Intake of 23.9 lbs. per day			
Digestible Energy	28,200 calories	Magnesium	10.9 g.
Crude Protein (10%)	1425 g.	Zinc	434 mg.
Calcium	56 g.	Copper	108 mg.
Phosphorus	36 g.	Vitamin A	29,940 IU

By the time the foal is weaned, the mare will probably be wondering how she ever let herself get into this predicament in the first place; she will be tired and worn, and will probably even be showing a few ribs. Just the same, you should cut back on the grain a week before and a week after weaning. This will help the foal adjust to being weaned, and will ensure that the mare is not turned out with a painfully full udder.

Nursing Foals

For a new foal, the act of being born is like awakening from a deep sleep inside a life-support incubator on a warm and cozy spaceship, and being cast naked onto a cold and hostile planet. Its supply of perfectly nourishing food has been severed, and it must very quickly learn to feed itself, or perish. For the first few days, it is content to drink its mother's milk, but after a week or so its curiosity leads it to sample the interesting selection of feeds its mother eats with such prejudicial single-mindedness.

Soon its inquisitiveness about Mother's food turns to desire, then to need. By three weeks of age the foal is growing so rapidly that its mother cannot possibly supply it with the nutrients it must have to continue this explosive stage of growth. If the mare is on pasture the foal can graze at will, and steal a little of whatever other feed the mare is getting. If the mare is penned up, the foal can eat as much hay as the mare will let it have. Either way, you now have to ask yourself if the foal is getting everything it needs to sustain its growth, or if extra feed—creep feed—sequestered away from the mare and available only to the foal, is necessary.

I know that many horsemen are opposed to creep feeding, and I can only suppose that they have had bad experiences of one kind or another, or simply have heard of someone who did. But I have creep fed hundreds of foals over the last 25 years, and have never seen one that was harmed in any way because of it. A foal that is given creep feed will grow 20% - 25% faster than one left to fend for itself, and if the ration is balanced it will suffer no ill-effects from this accelerated growth.

The goal of creep feeding is to give the foal the nutrients it is not getting enough of, not just to give it more food. To simply feed the foal more energy (as carbohydrates or fat) without meeting its protein or mineral requirements can, indeed, have unpleasant consequences. You could end up with a chubby foal on weak legs, with swollen joints, or worse. But with the right creep feed, you should see your investment paid back with interest. The question is: what does the foal need?

Daily Needs of 340 lb. 3 month-old Foal
(Adult Weight 1100 lb.)
Based on Total Dry Feed Intake of 12.1 lbs. per day

Digestible Energy	14,600 calories	Magnesium	4.0 g.
Crude Protein (10%)	730 g.	Zinc	230 mg.
Calcium	35 g.	Copper	65 mg.
Phosphorus	20 g.	Vitamin A	6940 IU

Although the foal is less than one-third the size of the maintenance horse, it needs 89% as much energy, 11% more protein, 75% more calcium, and 40% more phosphorus. How much of that is supplied by its mother's milk?

	Needed by Foal	Supplied in Milk	Deficit
Digestible Energy (Calories)	14,600	6,800	**7,800**
Crude Protein (grams)	730	250	**480**
Calcium (grams)	35	11	**24**
Phosphorus (grams)	20	7	**13**

Even after drinking 30 pounds of its mother's milk, the foal still needs more calcium, nearly as much phosphorus, and over half the protein and calories our 1100 pound maintenance horse needs. It would take a very accomplished sneak thief to steal that much nutrition away from a ravenous mother trying desperately to consume enough feed to keep up her end of the foal feeding program.

Supplying the foal with its source of feed is a simple enough thing to do. All it takes is a pen (creep feeder) that is accessible to the foal, but not the mare. The one I use is made from four panels constructed from 1½ inch pipe, 55 inches high. Three of the panels are 16 feet, the fourth is only 14 feet, the gap to the other panel being spanned with a single pipe on top. This leaves a 24" wide by 55" high opening the foal can easily walk through, but one that is too small for the mare. A round feeder placed in the middle of this enclosure contains the creep feed. A creep feeding pen of this size can easily accommodate six foals at a time.

Now all that is left is to determine what should go in the feeder. To do that, you should have a fair idea of the quality of forage the foal is getting. If you don't know, you should, at the very least, have your hay or pasture tested for digestible energy, protein, calcium, and phosphorus, since these are the most critical nutrients at this stage of the foal's life.

If you have good forage with plenty of energy and protein, there is no point in feeding a lot of extra energy if the foal doesn't need it. Check with your local feed mills to see what they have available. A partial guaranteed analysis of a 16% protein feed is included in the next section on weanlings and yearlings. Most feedmills carry comparable concentrates. Some feedmills carry 30% - 33% protein supplements that have less energy per pound and is fed at a much lower rate than the 16% feed. You may want to look at this type of supplement if you have good quality forage.

If the hay or pasture is more on the average side, you should offer the foal a less concentrated feed with a higher ratio of energy to protein, and feed more of it. A 14% or 16% protein feed, with 1,400 to 1,500 calories of digestible energy, is often fed at the rate of one pound per day, per month of age. This amount can be adjusted up or down, depending on the quality of forage. Many breeders offer creep feed free-choice, but most of the time the foal will only eat the recommended amount, anyway.

Feeds vary from area to area. The two important things to know are what your foal needs, and what it is getting from its forage and its mother's milk. Look in the section on weanlings and yearlings for a general analysis of several types of forage. Once you subtract what it is getting from what it needs, just add to the creep feeder what remains. If you have several foals, it should be no problem to get a feed mill to make a custom mix for you, if you provide them with an analysis of what you need.

WEANLINGS AND YEARLINGS

Next to the act of being born, weaning is the most stressful event in the young horse's life. It is also a stressful—and sleepless—time for the horseman who is not able to pen up the mares and foals beyond earshot of the bedroom window.

Even though the nutrient value of its mother's milk has slowly been declining, and the foal has been relying more and more on forages and concentrates for its nutritional needs, at weaning time a very large fraction is removed from the nutritional equation, and the foal will undoubtedly suffer some setback.

If the foal has been creep fed with a good quality concentrate, the drop in the foal's performance will be minimal, because the nutrition supplied from the mare's milk will not have been as nutritionally significant as with the non-creep fed foal. Nonetheless, after weaning, foals should be watched carefully for abnormalities of growth, gait, and general appearance, because this is the most probable time for nutritionally related problems to occur. The foal is, and has been, growing very quickly—by the time a foal is 6 months old it should have reached 45% of its adult weight, and 83% of its adult height. If the foal's body needs something it is in short supply of, it will not stop growing. Rather, it will simply use more of what is at hand. It is kind of like framing a wall with 1x8's when the plans call for 2x4's; you may get the wall built, but it is doubtful you will be happy with the results.

Although the nutritional requirements of the foal do not change on the day of weaning, the ration should change since the mare's milk has been removed from it. Let's look at the daily needs of a rapidly growing, 6 month-old weanling, and then decide how to meet those needs.

Daily Needs of 6 month-old Weanling
(Adult Weight 1100 lbs.)
Based on Total Dry Feed Intake of 14.5 lbs. per day

Digestible Energy	17,500 Calories	Magnesium	4.7 g.
Crude Protein (13.65%)	900 g.	Zinc	375 mg.
Calcium	38 g.	Copper	145 mg.
Phosphorus	22 g.	Vitamin A	11,000 IU

As always, these values are estimates, calculated for a weanling with a probable mature weight of 1100 pounds, and not unduly stressed by temperature extremes, disease, injury or parasites.

The table below lists the nutrient values for bluegrass pasture, and four different types of hay, on a dry matter basis. These values can vary substantially from region to region. If there are any peculiar soil conditions in your area that would affect the nutrient content of pasture or hay, your county extension agent would be able to tell you.

Typical Nutrient Values of Bluegrass Pasture and Hay

	Pasture	Alfalfa	Brome	Timothy	Orchard
DE (Cals/lb.)	950	940	850	800	880
Protein (g/lb.)	79	77	58	39	52
Calcium (g/lb.)	2.25	5.6	1.13	1.9	1.08
Phosphorus (g/lb.)	2.0	1.0	1.13	0.9	1.36
Zinc (mg/lb.)	13	12.7	11.8	17.3	16.3
Copper (mg/lb.)	7.1	7.3	10.0	6.4	7.6

The Fundamentals

Partial Analysis of Concentrated (16% Protein) Feed		
		As Shown on Feed Label
Digestible Energy	1440 Cal/lb.	*1.44 Mcals/lb.*
Protein (16%)	72.64 g/lb.	*16%*
Calcium	4.7 g/lb.	*1.03%*
Phosphorus	3.6 g/lb.	*0.79%*
Zinc	54.5 mg/lb.	*120 PPM*
Copper	18.2 mg/lb.	*40 PPM*

Now let's see where we are when we add concentrated feed to the ration. Below is a table giving the amounts of each of these nutrients found in 8 pounds of alfalfa/bromegrass hay and 6½ pounds of the 16% concentrate feed:

New Ration of Hay and Concentrated Feed
To Raise the Number of Calories and Nutrient Values

	4 lb. Alfalfa	4 lb. Brome	6.5 lb. Concentrate	18.5 lb. Total
DE (Calories)	3,760	3,400	9,360	**16,520**
Crude Protein (g.)	308.0	238.0	472.2	**1018.2**
Calcium (g.)	22.4	4.5	30.6	**57.5**
Phosphorus (g.)	4.0	4.5	23.4	**31.9**
Zinc (mg.)	50.8	47.2	354.1	**452.1**
Copper (mg.)	29.2	40.0	118.0	**187.2**

This is not in the least unwieldy. We are a little low in energy, a situation that could be remedied by the addition of corn oil, or full-fat extruded soybeans. The levels of zinc and copper are well within accepted limits, and should present no problems. There should also be enough phosphorus to balance the calcium. Of course, this is just a partial list of the nutrients needed by the weanling. The requirements for the other nutrients will be discussed under the individual vitamins and minerals.

As the weanling grows into a yearling, it will need more and more nutrients, but—since the volume of feed is now greater—the concentration of those nutrients is reduced.

Daily Needs of 12 month-old Yearling
(Adult Weight 1100 lbs.)
Based on Total Dry Feed Intake of 21.5 lbs. per day

Digestible Energy 22,500 Calories		Magnesium	7.5 g.
Crude Protein (11.25%)	1100 g.	Zinc	400 mg.
Calcium	39 g.	Copper	150 mg.
Phosphorus	21 g.	Vitamin A	16,000 IU

As shown by the above table, the feed for a yearling need not be as concentrated as that for the weanling. At 12 months the horse is eating half-again as much feed as the weanling, but only needs about a quarter more energy and protein, and just a little more calcium, phosphorus, zinc and copper. You might want to consider, at this point, feeding a less concentrated feed, such as a 14% mix, or even a 12% feed, if your hay is of good enough quality.

The goal should be to sustain steady growth. If you have made it this far without any major setbacks, you are well on your way to raising a healthy two-year-old.

Part Two

Nutrients That Don't Supply Energy

Chapter 6

ENZYMES: CATALYSTS OF LIFE

Though it is not my intention to give a short course on biological science, I will mention enzymes so often in the following pages that I thought it a subject worthy of expansion. It is included here because so many enzymes require minerals and vitamins for activation, and a short discussion of the importance of enzymes might further our appreciation of the vital roles of these nutrients.

While the temperature extremes on the earth's surface range between -128°F to 136°F, our bodies and those of our horses, must be maintained within a much smaller range. Yet many of the chemical reactions that take place within the body are very high-energy reactions that—when performed in the laboratory—require extremes of temperature and pressure that would kill us instantly. You cannot stir up starch and water in a test tube at 100 degrees Fahrenheit and expect to get sugar. So how do we do it?

The answer is enzymes. Enzymes are catalysts that are very specific for the reactions they facilitate. There are thousands of different enzymes in the body, each assigned to its own special task. They are proteins that rely on a very specific shape and configuration of atoms to work. But how do they work? The key is their shape, which is to say that their shapes are the keys. Whenever an enzyme binds two molecules together, or breaks the bond between them, it fits them together in a chemical embrace like a multi-dimensional key in an impossibly complex lock. Nearly every time a chemical bond is formed or broken—millions of times per second, in a horse—it is made possible by the presence of an enzyme. Without enzymes there would be neither digestion of food nor absorption of nutrients. Energy metabolism would grind to a halt. Growth and body maintenance would be impossible. And without minerals and vitamins, all of these enzymes would be immobilized.

Some of the Nutrients Involved In Enzyme Activity

Minerals	Vitamins
Calcium (Ca)	Riboflavin
Magnesium (Mg)	Niacin
Copper (Cu)	Pantothenic Acid
Manganese (Mn)	Pyridoxine
Zinc (Zn)	Biotin
Selenium (Se)	Thiamin

Minerals: Elemental Necessities

All of the nutrients we have discussed to this point consist almost exclusively of carbon, hydrogen, oxygen and nitrogen which, interestingly, are all components of common atmospheric gases: carbon dioxide (CO_2), water vapor (H_2O) and nitrogen gas (N_2). Does this mean a horse derives its energy out of thin air? Well not directly, but it is interesting to note that about 93 percent of the dry mass of green plants is derived not from the soil, but from the atmosphere. Plants—with the help of sunlight and water—<u>do</u> turn air into food, and in that sense we could say that what is energy for the horse today was thin air yesterday.

Now we dip further into the periodic table to the more earthy elements known as minerals. There is not much that goes on in the horse's body without the assistance of minerals. Without minerals, the carbohydrates, fats and proteins in the feed could not be converted into muscle, blood, bone or ligaments. Most vitamins, which act as catalysts in the body, require minerals to work.

A horse receiving an ample supply of minerals will require less feed and perform at a higher level than one that is not. It will have a greater resistance to disease. Energy levels and reproductive efficiency will be increased. Mares will cycle earlier in the year, conceive more quickly, and be more apt to carry their foals to term.

They will produce more milk, their foals will grow larger, faster, and will exhibit stronger, denser bone.

Plants do not absorb minerals from the atmosphere, although some minerals, such as sulfur and phosphorus, are part of certain gases found in the air. Minerals are unique among the nutrients. Since they are elements, they are indestructible (except at nuclear energies far beyond the range of horse and horseman). Yet even though they cannot be destroyed in the way that carbohydrates, fats, and proteins can, minerals can be moved from place to place, like from the hayfield to the muck bucket, and often they do not find their way back (more on this later). Many minerals act exactly like vitamins, since they are part of enzymes or coenzymes, but minerals are elemental and inorganic, while vitamins are organic compounds made up primarily from the atmospheric gases we mentioned earlier. Vitamins can be manufactured, minerals cannot— they can only be found, or lost.

In the following pages you will see, again and again, that too much of one mineral will interfere with the absorption of another. Minerals must be balanced in the ration. If they are not, a cascading effect of imbalances may occur and virtually every system in the body will be affected. The horse has relatively high tolerance ranges for some minerals, such as copper and zinc. Other minerals, like iron and selenium, are not so forgiving. The prudent horseman will always consider individual minerals in context to every other mineral in the ration. It may not be easy, but the results will be well-worth the trouble.

The reference chart on page 85 give the daily mineral requirements for several classes of the horse, and should be a useful guide for those who are considering supplemental minerals.

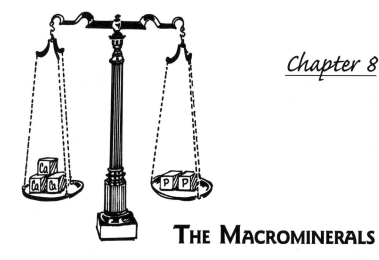

THE MACROMINERALS

O f the over twenty minerals known to be needed by the horse, seven are termed macrominerals, because they are needed in relatively large quantities. The remaining are termed microminerals, or simply trace minerals (or trace elements), since they are needed in only trace amounts. The seven macrominerals are: calcium, phosphorus, magnesium, sodium and chloride (salt), potassium, and sulfur.

CALCIUM (Ca) AND PHOSPHORUS (P)
Searching for the Illusive Balance.

Short of beating your horse's legs with a shovel, there is really no better way to ruin a good, young horse, than to feed it a diet with a skewed calcium to phosphorus ratio. I have talked to and corresponded with hundreds of horse owners over the years who had problems caused by an imbalance of calcium and phosphorus; and almost invariably, their problem was the result of too much calcium in relation to the phosphorus they were feeding. The most common symptom is swollen knees and fetlock joints in young horses, a condition usually referred to as epiphysitis, or simply physitis. It is a result of a pathological transformation of cartilage into bone. Epiphysitis can be caused by either too much phosphorus or calcium, though calcium is the usual culprit. If the problem is not too far advanced, balancing the calcium and phosphorus in the diet will reverse the symptoms in a few weeks. Occasionally, a mare will produce so much milk that the high calcium content will induce a case of epiphysitis. If this occurs, the mare's energy ration should be cut back to slow milk production and/or the foal should be supplemented with phosphorus. If possible, it might be advisable to wean the foal early.

Feeding too little calcium can be every bit as dangerous, causing conditions known as rickets, where the skeleton becomes weak and deformed, or Miller's Disease (Big Head Disease) where the bones of the face, particularly along the jaws and nasal passages, become enlarged. The point is, horses need lots of both calcium and phosphorus, and in a ratio that does not supply too much of one over the other.

What is the magic ratio, and why is it so hard to reach it? Well, conventional wisdom holds that a 2:1 ratio of calcium to phosphorus in the feed is a safe number to go with, and if we need a number to hang our hat on, that is as good as any. According to the NRC (National Research Council), adult horses can tolerate a ratio as high as 5:1, while growing horses are not harmed by a 3:1 ratio. These ratios are workable, providing that there is sufficient phosphorus in the diet. On the other hand, I know of no horse that ever suffered any harm from calcium or phosphorus when given adequate amounts within the 1:1 to 2:1 range, and the NRC suggests that this is the optimum range.

Why is it so hard to reach a ratio of such broad tolerance? A look at what many horsemen feed their horses should shed some light on the problem. Most horsemen feed alfalfa hay, or an alfalfa/grass mix. Hay is the major part of the diet, and alfalfa hay is a major source of calcium. Some alfalfa hay is as much as eight times richer in calcium than phosphorus, and a 6:1 ratio is not at all uncommon.

Cereal grains, such as oats, corn and barley, on the other hand, usually favor phosphorus by 2:1. The problem is, most horses are fed a lot more hay than grain, and grain contains so little of each that it can do little to reestablish a balance.

Supplement manufacturers do little to help the situation. They are well aware of the coveted 2:1 ratio, and most supplements are formulated accordingly, rather than taking into account the excess calcium coming from most hays. Unfortunately, horses (and dogs and cats) are forced to ride the tides of human nutritional fads and, for reasons I can only imagine, calcium has become the darling of food manufacturers, while phosphorus is thought to be something wooden matches are made from. It is no exaggeration to say that every time someone on Wall Street touts the value of an antacid with calcium, a young horse suffers.

The Functions of Calcium

A horse's body is about 2% calcium, while the skeleton is almost 35% calcium. Calcium is absorbed more efficiently by the body than most other minerals, including phosphorus. Absorption rates vary between 50% - 70%, with the ability to absorb calcium declining with age. Calcium from inorganic sources, such as dicalcium phosphate or limestone[1] (calcium carbonate) are better absorbed than from the organic sources found in forages and grains. Calcium absorption can be negatively affected by excess phosphorus, and oxalate, a compound found in most plants in small quantities. Russian Thistle, which grows well in hay fields and often ends up in hay, can contain toxic amounts of oxalate. Phytate, a substance found in many plants, can also reduce calcium absorption. This is especially important for those who like to give their horses bran mashes, since bran is high in phytate.

---

1 Limestone is, technically speaking, an organic compound, since it contains the element carbon. However, since the calcium is not bound to an organic substrate, such as an amino acid, protein, or polysaccharide, it is considered inorganic within the feed industry.

Besides its major role in bone formation, calcium is also required for:

- Muscular contraction
- Blood clotting
- Normal release of hormones
- Activation of enzymes
- Normal heart rhythm

Below are some common grains and forages and the amount of each that should contain around 22 grams of calcium:

To get 22 grams of calcium, you would need to feed one of the following each day:	
Alfalfa hay (1.24% calcium)	3.9 pounds
Timothy hay (0.43%)	11.3 pounds
Bromegrass hay (0.25% calcium)	19.4 pounds
Oats (0.08% calcium)	60.6 pounds
Corn (0.05% calcium)	97.0 pounds
Barley (0.05% calcium)	97.0 pounds

As I said earlier, cereal grains do not have an abundance of calcium! Conversely, alfalfa hay is loaded with it, so if you are feeding alfalfa hay, and a lot of it, it would be wise to either feed some grass hay along with it, or to supplement with a good source of inorganic phosphorus (preferably monosodium phosphate, which is 26% phosphorus, and supplies 7.37 grams of phosphorus per ounce). On the other hand, if you are feeding grass hay with plenty of grain, you may have to supplement calcium with an inorganic source, such as limestone or dicalcium phosphate.

The Functions of Phosphorus

While most of the phosphorus a horse absorbs goes into the skeleton (which is 14% - 17% phosphorus), phosphorus is needed for many other functions in the body, including:

- Fat and Carbohydrate metabolism
- Repair and growth of cells
- Production of Energy (ATP)
- Calcium and sugar metabolism

- Utilization of vitamins
- Kidney function
- Muscle activity

Phosphorus is not as easily absorbed as calcium. A good estimate for the absorption rate of phosphorus is in the range of 30% - 55%. Like calcium, phosphorus is absorbed better by younger horses than mature horses, and is more likely to be absorbed if it is derived from an inorganic source, such as monosodium phosphate. Most phosphorus absorption takes place in the hindgut, with the assistance of bacteria. Therefore, the absorption of phosphorus can be assisted by the addition to the feed of certain bacteria enhancing agents, such as yeast culture, or by feeding the bacteria culture, itself (e.g., lactobacillus acidophilus). It may not be advisable to feed the bacteria culture for extended periods of time, but rather only to debilitated horses, or horses under severe stress. There is no point in doing for the horse what the horse can normally do for itself.

Below is how much it would take of each of these grains and forages to supply 14 grams of phosphorus. The far right column shows what percentage of the maintenance level 22 gram calcium requirement is supplied by each of these feeds.

**To get 14 grams of phosphorus,
you would need to feed one of the following each day:**

Alfalfa hay (.22% phosphorus)	14 pounds	(359% Calcium*)
Timothy hay (.20%)	15 pounds	(132% Calcium*)
Bromegrass hay (.25%)	12 pounds	(62% Calcium*)
Oats (.34%)	9 pounds	(15% Calcium*)
Corn (.27%)	11 pounds	(12% Calcium*)
Barley (.34%)	9 pounds	(10% Calcium*)

*Percent of Calcium Requirement, based on 22 grams/day.

Obviously, it takes a very large amount of grain to supply enough phosphorus to balance out the calcium in alfalfa hay; probably more than most horsemen need to feed. A sensible way to overcome this problem would be to feed some grass hay along with the alfalfa and/or to include a source of inorganic phosphorus in the grain ration.

Calcium & Phosphorus Requirements

Following are some guidelines for the dietary calcium and phosphorus requirements for different classes of horses. They should be used as rules of thumb, not as proclamations carved in granite. As pointed out above, there are many factors that would invoke a necessity to feed more or less calcium and phosphorus. These amounts were calculated assuming a horse of 1100 pounds mature weight.

Daily Needs of Calcium & Phosphorus	Calcium	Phosphorus
Maintenance Horse	22 g.	14 g.
Pregnant Mare - 1st & 2nd trimester	22 g.	14 g.
Pregnant Mare - 3rd trimester	38 g.	28 g.
Lactating Mare	56 g.	36 g.
Nursing foal, 3 months	35 g.	20 g.
Weanling, 6 months	38 g.	21 g.
Yearling, 12 months	39 g.	22 g.
Yearling in training, 18 months	40 g.	23 g.
Lightly Working Horse	25 g.	18 g.
Moderately Working Horse	30 g.	21 g.
Intensely Working Horse	40 g.	28 g.
Breeding Stallion	25 g.	18 g.

How important is the calcium/phosphorus ratio?

A friend of yours has just bought a little place in Colorado. He has a few horses and he says the best alfalfa hay in the world is grown there. He feeds it to all of his horses, including the young ones. They eat up to 18 pounds per day, plus he gives each of them a couple of pounds of oats. Then one day he calls to tell you that all of his youngsters' legs are swollen and puffy in the knees and fetlock joints. They can hardly walk. What should he do?

You do a few calculations and estimate that he is feeding 102 grams of calcium to 21 grams of phosphorus, nearly a 5:1 ratio, which is unacceptable for his young horses. You tell him to find some grass hay to mix with his alfalfa, to lower the total hay intake and make up the difference with more grain. And finally you tell him to add 2 ounces of monosodium phosphate to the diet.

Since you were shooting from the hip, you really didn't take the time to refigure his diet. So as you set down the phone, you put a pencil to it and come up with the following results:

Feed	Amount Fed	Calcium	Phosphorus
Alfalfa	8 lbs.	45.0 g.	8.0 g.
Timothy	8 lbs.	15.0 g.	7.0 g.
Oats	4 lbs.	1.5 g.	6.0 g.
Monosodium phosphate	0.22 lbs	0.0 g.	12.5 g.
TOTALS	**20.22 lbs**	**61.5 grams**	**33.5 grams**

Not bad: the ratio is now down below 2:1, and even though your friend is still feeding large amounts of calcium, he now has enough phosphorus to balance it. A month later he calls and tells you that you are a genius. He says that all of his young horses are normal now, and running around like so many banshees. You say that you knew they would be, and you thank him for following your advice, as you pat yourself on the back.

As hard as it may be to believe, this little drama is played all too frequently, and often with far less satisfying results. Many horses are destroyed each year as a result of unwise feeding programs, horses that could be living long and healthy lives if just a few corrections were made to their diets, in a timely fashion.

Magnesium (Mg)

A horse's body contains about .05% magnesium, of which 60% is found in the skeleton and the teeth. This means that the body of the average horse has a little more than ½ pound of magnesium in its tissues. Although magnesium is a major player in the chemistry of life, it is a nutrient we usually do not hear too much about, because most grains and forages have enough magnesium to supply the needs of most horses. Magnesium is contained in the chlorophyll of green plants, a fact that ensures it to have a fairly even distribution in the natural elements of a horse's diet. Typically, this is between 0.1% - 0.3% of dry matter.

The requirement for horses ranges from about 7.5 grams per day for a maintenance horse, to 15.1 grams per day for a horse in heavy training. Since a maintenance horse will eat about 18 - 20 pounds of dry matter per day, even if we use the lower figure for the amount of magnesium found in natural feed, (0.1%) we see that enough magnesium—a little over 8 grams—is present in the diet. However, the horse in heavy training that is eating 25 to 30 pounds of dry matter per day will only obtain about 12 or 13 grams of magnesium from a diet that contains 0.10% - 0.11% magnesium. Such feeds include corn, and bromegrass, timothy, and orchardgrass hays. Oats and barley have a little more magnesium, with an average analysis showing concentrations of 0.16% and 0.14%, respectively. And, as you might imagine, alfalfa hay tops the list of common feeds, with 0.30% - 0.35% magnesium. A performance horse, therefore, that is receiving 10 pounds of alfalfa hay and 6 pounds each of oats and corn should be getting enough magnesium (about 24 grams). But if we substitute the alfalfa with a grass hay, the magnesium total is only around 14 grams; a little low.

In the body, magnesium is needed for the synthesis of proteins, and the digestion of starches. It is also an activator for many enzymes. Deficiencies of magnesium can cause nervousness and muscle tremors and eventually mineralization in the arteries and damaged capillaries. A horse receiving low levels of dietary magnesium will have a rough, lusterless haircoat. A horse receiving adequate magnesium will require less energy to perform the same amount of work as a horse receiving suboptimal levels of magnesium.

Magnesium in the feed is absorbed at a rate of 40% - 60%. Inorganic forms of magnesium, such as magnesium sulfate and magnesium oxide, are generally about 70% absorbed by the horse. However, several factors can limit magnesium absorption, including high levels of calcium or phosphorus in the diet; an excess of vitamin D; diuretics, such as Lasix; and a lack of dietary protein.

Many horses that are getting what should be adequate amounts of magnesium in the diet do, nonetheless, display symptoms of low magnesium, such as muscle tremors. Most of these horses respond to the introduction of supplemental magnesium to the feed, in the form of magnesium oxide or magnesium sulfate.

SULFUR (S)

The depth of the controversy surrounding the mineral sulfur is exceeded only by our lack of knowledge about just what sulfur does in the body. In this section I will present the facts that are known about sulfur, and reserve the controversy for the section on MSM in Chapter 12, "Exotic Nutrients".

Sulfur accounts for about 0.15% of a horse's mass, which means that the body of the average horse contains a little more than 1½ pounds of sulfur. Most of this is contained in the hooves and the hair, which are both around 3% sulfur. There are two amino acids that contain sulfur: methionine and cystine. Methionine is an essential amino acid that must be present in the diet. Cystine is not considered to be an essential amino acid, as long as there is plenty of methionine, since the body can easily synthesize the former from the latter. (Except for the addition of one sulfur atom and one hydrogen atom, cystine is identical to the major portion of the methionine molecule.)

In addition, sulfur is present in the vitamins biotin and thiamin (B_1), insulin (which regulates blood sugar), heparin (an anticoagulant), and chondroitin sulfate, a major constituent of joint and connective tissue.

Sulfur gets around. By going through the list of nutrients that contain sulfur, we can see that without it a horse would be quite a mess. It could not metabolize carbohydrates or even simple blood sugar. Hooves and hair could not grow, blood could not flow, and joints would not move. Not that any of this makes much difference, because without sulfur a horse would literally fall apart at the seams, since it is the disulfide bond in cystine that gives protein its shape.

Yet I cannot tell you just how much sulfur a horse needs, because no one really knows a horse's sulfur requirement. We do know that a good quality protein source will contain about 0.15% sulfur, and this appears to be enough for most horses. Many veterinarians and farriers suggest supplementation of methionine and biotin for horses with foot and hoof problems, and in many cases this is sound advice, although if the goal is simply to provide your horse with more sulfur, methionine is far and away the cheaper of the two. In olden times raw sulfur was fed as a means to improve and maintain hoof quality, and to some extent this practice is used today. Elemental sulfur, however, is not a natural nutrient, and its liberal use should be cautioned against.

How much sulfur is too much? Again, its hard to say, but certainly more than the prudent horseman is likely to feed. It is known that excess sulfur can inhibit copper absorption in ruminants, but this has not been seen in horses.

Potassium (K)

Potassium is an important mineral in the regulation of osmotic pressure, and the acid-base balance within the body. Osmotic pressure is controlled by potassium and sodium working together to regulate the fluid content within the cells of the body. Potassium also plays a role in the transmission of nerve impulses, and in proper muscle function. Many horses suffering from Azoturia (tying up) have been found to have low levels of potassium, calcium and/or sodium, and have responded favorably to the introduction of higher levels of these minerals into the diet. Horses deficient in potassium will lose their appetites, and eventually refuse to eat. Weight loss and a generally poor appearance can be the result of a diet low in potassium.

Forages are relatively high in potassium, while cereal grains are lacking. Alfalfa hay on the average will be around 1.40% potassium. Grass hays will range from 1.60% - 2.90%, with orchardgrass topping the list. Oats, corn and barley all fall in between 0.30% - 0.45%.

The potassium requirements of different classes of adult horses range from about 25 grams per day for an 1100 pound maintenance horse, to 50 grams per day for a horse in heavy training. Lactating mares need nearly as much as horses in heavy training (around 46 grams), while a mare in the last month of pregnancy will only need 31 grams per day. The amount of potassium needed by young horses (with an estimated adult weight of 1100 pounds) ranges from 15 grams per day for a 6 month-old weanling, to 28 grams per day for an 18 month-old horse in training.

Horses whose diets consist primarily of hay or pasture should not need any additional potassium. A horse eating 14 pounds of average hay, for example, would be getting over 95 grams of potassium. On the other hand, horses on high grain diets and/or horses that sweat profusely, such as race horses or endurance horses, probably should be given extra potassium. Potassium chloride is very inexpensive and can be readily added as a top dressing on the feed. There are also several good electrolyte formulas on the market that contain potassium. They can either be added to the feed, or dissolved in water.

SALT (SODIUM CHLORIDE - NaCl)

No matter what you are feeding, it is very doubtful that it contains enough salt, unless it was added at the feed mill. Grains and forages do not provide enough sodium or chloride to maintain most horses, so it should always be offered free choice, either loose, or in a block, and <u>always</u> with abundant water nearby. Salt blocks can be straight salt, iodized salt, or mineralized salt that contains many important trace minerals.

Sodium and chloride help maintain the acid-base balance within the body, and assist in the osmotic regulation of body fluids. Sodium acts in concert with potassium to regulate the fluid content of cells; potassium keeps the cells from drying out, while sodium keeps them from filling with water.

Horses not getting enough salt will eat slower than normal, and will drink less water. They will develop rough haircoats and dry skin. Often they will develop the habit of licking, especially things that have dried sweat on them, such as shovel handles.

Since so much salt is lost in sweat, the requirement for it increases in proportion to the amount of work a horse is doing. While a maintenance horse might get by with 8 or 9 grams of sodium per day and a lactating mare will only need 10 to 12 grams, a horse in heavy training will require 35 to 40 grams per day. For horse in training, loose salt is preferable to a block. It takes 102 grams of salt to supply 40 grams of sodium, and that makes for a lot of licking!

Quick Summary of Macrominerals

- **Calcium** is plentiful in hay, especially alfalfa hay.
- Alfalfa hays often have Ca to P ratios of 5:1 or 6:1, but can be as high as 8:1.
- Cereal grains have more **phosphorus** than **calcium**.
- It is much easier to feed too much **calcium**, than too much **phosphorus**.
- **Calcium** is absorbed with 55% - 70% efficiency.
- **Phosphorus** is absorbed with 30% - 55% efficiency.
- **Calcium** and **phosphorus** are more easily absorbed from inorganic sources.
- The maximum tolerable **calcium** to **phosphorus** ratio for mature horses is 5:1; for growing horses, 3:1. The optimum ratio is between 1:1 and 2:1.
- **Magnesium** from grains and forages is 40% - 60% absorbed, while inorganic, supplemental forms are about 70% absorbed.
- **Magnesium** is needed for protein synthesis, starch digestion, and the functioning of enzymes.
- Grains and forages usually contain enough **magnesium** for most horses.
- **Sulfur** is needed for sugar and carbohydrate metabolism, and it is present in many key compounds in the body.
- No dietary minimum requirement has been established for **sulfur**, although its importance in the body is well recognized.
- The amino acid, methionine, is the most common source of dietary **sulfur**.
- Horses are tolerant of large amounts of **sulfur**.
- Forages are high in **potassium**; cereal grains are low.
- **Sodium** is lacking in most common feeds.
- **Potassium** and **salt** are lost in sweat, increasing the requirement in working horses.
- **Potassium** chloride is inexpensive and can easily be added to the grain.
- **Salt** should always be offered free choice, with plenty of water.

_____ *Macrominerals*

Chapter 9

TRACE MINERALS

Trace minerals are essential for life, but needed in smaller quantities than the macrominerals. They are all further down on the periodic table than the macrominerals, which means they are heavier and generally less abundant in nature than their more ubiquitous counterparts.

Another curious difference is that most trace minerals are absorbed better when they are part of an organic substrate, while the macrominerals are better absorbed in inorganic form. Sodium chloride, potassium chloride, magnesium oxide, monosodium phosphate, dicalcium phosphate; all of these inorganic compounds deliver minerals more efficiently to the body than their organic counterparts (though I may get some dissenting opinions in the case of magnesium). The exception is sulfur, which is virtually unavailable to the body when supplied in inorganic forms. Of the seven trace minerals under discussion here, (cobalt, copper, iodine, iron, manganese, selenium and zinc) only one (selenium) is better absorbed in its inorganic forms.

Trace minerals are vitally important to the health of your horse. The fact that they are needed in such small quantities should not undermine their essential metabolic roles. The important thing to remember is that nature always builds with the materials she has at hand. It is no coincidence that the energy supplying nutrients—carbohydrates, fats and proteins—are all composed of atmospheric gases, and neither is it coincidence that trace minerals have been incorporated into the process of life in amounts commensurate with their abundance in the soil.

What if certain soils—namely farmland—were to slowly become depleted in certain of the elements necessary to sustain life? Unfortunately, this is happening—has been happening—for quite a few years.

In the past, before urbanization and the widespread distribution of farm products, all of the minerals brought up from the soil by grasses, trees, and other vegetation, were returned to it. The soil was nourished by the wastes and the bodies of the animals that lived and died upon it. But times have changed. Today, Colorado beef grown on Iowa corn is shipped to South America. Much of Nebraska's wheat ends up on a slow boat to Russia. North Dakota oats nourish horses between Florida and California. As all of these products leave the areas where they were produced, the minerals they contain go with them—on a one-way ticket.

Additionally, midwestern and southern farmland that receives high levels of rainfall each year is subject to leaching of trace minerals. (Leaching is the loss of nutrients by water washing them from the soil.) Irrigated fields undergo similar losses. Over many years, these elements are lost which causes forages and grains to be deficient in these important nutrients.

Farmers fertilize with nitrogen, phosphorus and potassium, and occasionally calcium, but that leaves 18 to 20 minerals essential to horses (and horsemen) that are not being returned to the ground. Since plants don't require the high levels of minerals that animals need in order to thrive, even perfectly healthy-looking grains and forages often cannot supply the levels of minerals our horses require.

The demineralization of our soil is not the slow process we

might imagine. Tests done on dehydrated alfalfa meal by the National Academy of Sciences between 1973 and 1981 yielded some disturbing results. Copper dropped from 11.2 PPM down to 9.5 PPM during that period. Iron went from 330 PPM to 270 PPM, and zinc fell from 21.5 PPM to 19.4 PPM. These figures represent losses of 15%, 18% and 10%, respectively, in less than a decade.

ORGANIC VS. INORGANIC TRACE MINERALS

The depletion of our soils is a phenomenon well-known to the feed industry. Most feed and supplement manufacturers fortify their products with minerals. Every year, millions of tons of ground ores, in the forms of oxides, sulfates, and carbonates, are processed and added to feed, food, and supplements for domestic animals and humans. But how good are they?

As we have already seen, inorganic macrominerals are generally quite efficient, even better than organic forms in most cases. But inorganic trace minerals are not nearly as well absorbed. Once a trace mineral becomes disassociated from the salt (sulfate, carbonate, etc.) it was bound to, it takes on a positive charge, which binds it like a magnet to the negatively charged intestinal wall, thus denying it passage into the cells.

Organic minerals, in contrast to inorganic sulfate, oxide and carbonate forms, are either electrically neutral, or have only a slight negative charge. This neutrality is the primary reason organic trace minerals are better absorbed. There are two general categories of organic minerals: complexes, and chelates and proteinates.

Complexes

Complexes can be either in polysaccharide or amino acid form. In polysaccharide complexes the mineral is encapsulated, or "sequestered" in a coating of giant sea kelp. Polysaccharide complexes are not organic in the true sense of the word, since the mineral (usually in sulfate form) is not chemically bound to the polysaccharide substrate. They owe their effectiveness to the fact that the complex is largely protected from the digestive process until it reaches the intestine, where the substrate dissolves and the metal ion can then undergo a natural chelation process that will greatly facilitate its passage through the intestinal lining. Amino acid complexes tend to be a little more stable than the polysaccharide forms. Otherwise they react similarly to improve trace mineral bio-availability. One major advantage of complexes over simple inorganic sulfates is the fact that they do not usually react with fragile vita-mins in feeds and supplements. This can greatly improve vitamin stability in such products.

Chelates and Proteinates

In contrast to complexes, chelates and proteinates are chemically bound, through a commercial process, to specific amino acid or protein digest fragments, before they ever get into your horse's feed. The term chelate (pronounced KEY-late) is derived from the Latin word "chelae", which literally means "scorpion claws". The analogy is an apt one if we imagine a scorpion holding a BB between the tips of its claws. Chemically, a chelate is a five or six-sided ring containing a positively-charged metal ion. The metal ion is held fast within the ring by negatively charged electrons. A true chelate will have two or more points of attachment to the metal ion, which improves the stability.

The difference between chelated and proteinated minerals is subtle. By definition, a chelate is an entity in which the metal ion is chemically bound to a known combination of amino acids, whereas a proteinate is a chelate consisting of amino acids or partially hydro-lyzed protein. Proteinates are more difficult to manufacture properly, cost more to produce, but may be more effective than straight chelates.

Feeding Organic Minerals

The manufacturers of polysaccharide complexes recommend that they be fed just as though they were regular sulfates, oxides and carbonates. While they are considerably more efficient than regular inorganic trace minerals, they are not bullet-proof, and they leave the body of the horse some degree of discretion over what to absorb, and what not to.

Chelates, and especially proteinates, are extremely effective organic entities that are so well absorbed that a serious mineral imbalance could result from their misuse. For that reason, the manufacturers recommend that chelates and proteinates should only comprise 20% - 33% of the total trace mineral content added to the feed, the difference being made up with inorganic minerals.

Since trace minerals are so important, serious horsemen should consider adding organic trace minerals to their horses rations, if extra minerals are needed. Performance and breeding horses are especially responsive to the addition of organic trace minerals to their diets.

Organic Forms	Inorganic Forms
Polysaccharide Complex	Sulfate
Amino Acid Complex	Oxide
Chelate	Carbonate
Proteinate	Phosphate
Chloride	

THE TRACE ELEMENTS

Cobalt (Co)

The mineral cobalt is necessary for the synthesis of vitamin B_{12}, which in turn is needed for the formation of hemoglobin. This is the solitary known function of cobalt. The minimum requirements for cobalt have not been thoroughly studied, but a range from 0.8 milligrams per day for a maintenance horse, to 1.4 milligrams per day for a growing horse in training are considered adequate. A cobalt deficiency can cause anemia, reduced appetite, and a slowed rate of growth.

Forages generally contain 0.09 - 0.16 mg./lb. of cobalt, while grains have between 0.025 - 0.22 mg./lb., though these amounts can vary from place to place. A horse eating 14 pounds of feed with an average cobalt content of 0.10 mg./lb. would, therefore, be getting enough. Cobalt is usually included in small quantities in mineral blocks and supplements.

Copper (Cu)

The body of the horse puts copper to work in a number of places. It is needed for many of the enzyme systems involved in the manufacture and maintenance of connective tissue, utilization of iron, maintenance of mitochondria within the cell nucleus, and the synthesis of the pigment melanin. Copper is also required for bone formation, maintaining the elastic strength of blood vessels, the manufacture of hemoglobin, and the healing of wounds. Copper is especially important for maintaining an efficient immune system.

Like all minerals, copper must be in a proper balance with other macro and microminerals. A deficiency of copper can result from a diet too high in calcium, iron, molybdenum and zinc, and also by a diet low in protein. Horses fed a copper deficient diet—or a diet high in copper limiting nutrients—may develop enlarged joints and fragile bones. Their growth will be slowed and they may become anemic. Osteochondrosis, or metabolic bone disease, may result from a prolonged copper deficiency.

The minimum requirements for dietary copper range from 80 milligrams per day for the maintenance horse, to 150 milligrams per day for a yearling in training, though optimum amounts may be somewhat higher. Horses can tolerate much higher levels of copper than the minimum requirement.

Forages usually contain between 4 - 11 mg./lb. of copper, but the availability of copper in forages is only in the 6% - 34% range. Grass hays are generally higher in copper than alfalfa hay. Grains have less copper than forages, with amounts ranging from 1.6 mg./lb. for corn to 3.7 mg./lb. for barley. Most feed, therefore, does not contain enough copper for most horses—especially horses on high carbohydrate diets—and some degree of supplementation would be beneficial.

Iodine (I)

Most of us have never seen a person or animal with a goiter (a condition in which the thyroid gland becomes so swollen that a large unsightly protrusion develops on the neck), and we have iodized salt to thank for that fact. Goiters were common in people, livestock and pets until the first part of this century, when it was discovered that dietary iodine would cure goiters and reverse other symptoms of low thyroid activity.

The thyroid gland, which is responsible for regulating the rate of metabolism, produces two amino acid-like hormones (thyroxine and triiodothyronine) that both contain iodine. When there is too little iodine in the diet, the gland is stimulated by a different hormone that causes it to swell. Thyroid hormones can be thought of as metronomes for the body. They determine the rate at which the body consumes oxygen, burns glucose, and synthesizes protein.

Though mature horses seldom develop goiters, they are common in foals born to iodine-deficient mares. Such foals will have trouble standing to nurse, and will appear to be very weak. Mares that are deficient in iodine may have abnormal estrous cycles. Other symptoms include rough haircoats, brittle hooves and sparse hair.

The minimum iodine requirement is estimated at 0.1 PPM in the diet. Some common feedstuffs can contain as much as 2 PPM iodine, while others contain none, at all, depending on where they were grown. Many areas of the United States have iodine-deficient soil, particularly in the Great Lakes Basin, as well as a number of Midwestern, western, and northern states. (The first test to determine if supplemental iodine would cure goiters was conducted in Cleveland in 1916.) But there is no need to have your feed tested for iodine, since iodized salt—salt that contains 70 PPM of iodine—is available for the same price as the regular salt you should already be giving your horse free-choice.

Iron (Fe)

Most of what iron does in the body is related to the transport of oxygen to the cells, which means there is little that goes on in the body that does not involve iron. Its most notable presence is in the hemoglobin molecule, the primary constituent of the red blood cell where, in the average horse, 60% of the body's 33 grams of iron can be found. It is also a component of myoglobin, a hemoglobin-like compound that loosely holds oxygen in the muscles when it is abundant, and releases it when the body needs it.

Iron is a mineral the horseman needs to be careful with. There are probably more problems caused by an overabundance of iron, than by a lack of it. Even though the absorption rate is low—between 10% - 15% —grains and forages generally contain enough iron for the needs of most horses. Exceptions would include horses under stress; horses that have lost a lot of blood from injuries; and horses stressed by heavy parasitic loads. High levels of cadmium, cobalt, copper, zinc and manganese can also limit iron absorption.

The minimum iron requirement* for a maintenance horse is 40 PPM, or about 18.14 milligrams in each pound of feed. Growing foals, late pregnant and lactating mares should have more on the order of 50 PPM in the entire ration, which works out to about 22.68 milligrams in each pound of feed. Most common feeds contain at least 65 PPM, with a few exceptions, such as corn and timothy hay, which usually contain less than 40 PPM. Alfalfa hay, on the other hand, often contains more than 200 PPM of iron. Since iron is so well conserved in the body, iron supplementation should not be necessary for most horses, though the judicious addition of iron to the diets of young, fast growing horses, lactating or pregnant mares, and performance horses, can be beneficial.

Myths about iron are rife in the performance horse community. It is a belief held by some race horse trainers that feeding outrageous amounts of iron—or injecting it—will enhance the production of red blood cells, which in turn will increase the packed cell volume and augment the blood's capacity for carrying oxygen. Often the outcome is the opposite of the desired effect: a tired, fatigued horse that can't seem to keep weight on.

High levels of iron will lower the amount of available zinc and copper, which in turn can lead to other mineral imbalances. It can also adversely affect the metabolism of phosphorus, which can result in a slowed rate of growth accompanied by poorly mineralized bone. Also, many pathogenic bacteria have a high requirement for iron. Thus, excess iron may make bacterial infections worse.

Most popular liquid "iron tonics" contain a daily dose of 450 to 550 milligrams of iron, in widely varying forms. The better ones also include balanced amounts of other important trace minerals along with a full spectrum of vitamins. Many successful trainers swear by these products, and some of the better products certainly can be beneficial to high-powered horses under a lot of stress. On the other hand, there are a few "jug" products that are not worth the cost of the bottle they come in. As with most everything, you get what you pay for.

Manganese (Mn)

Not much attention was given to manganese by horsemen until recently, when chondroitin sulfate supplements became so popular. Chondroitin sulfate is one of the main constituents of joint cartilage, and manganese is required by the enzymes that facilitate its utilization. Manganese is also needed for carbohydrate and fat metabolism, and for normal reproductive function.

Little work has been done to establish the manganese requirement for horses, but it is generally believed that 40 PPM in the diet is adequate. Timothy hay and orchardgrass hay both contain more than that—50 PPM and 140 PPM respectively—but most other common feeds are lacking. Alfalfa hay contains around 25 PPM manganese (and lower amounts when the calcium level is high), oats have around 36 PPM, barley 16 PPM, and corn bottoms the list with only 5 PPM. Some degree of supplementation, therefore, should be a consideration, especially for growing horses and performance horses.

Since manganese is so vitally important for the formation of connective tissues, foals born to mares deficient in manganese may have crooked legs and deformed joints with severely limited articulation. Performance horses not receiving enough manganese will exhibit stiff joints and general soreness, and will not want to work.

Just as the minimum requirements for this mineral are not fully known, neither is the level of toxicity, but at the very least, an excess in the diet should interfere with the absorption and utilization of other nutrients.

Zinc (Zn)

Zinc is another mineral that really gets around. It is found in high concentrations in the eye and the prostate gland, as well as in the skin, hair and hooves. It is essential for the functioning of several (as many as 340) enzyme systems, which adds greatly to its importance in the body. Among the many functions of zinc, it is needed for skin growth and healing, normal prostate function, and phosphorus and protein metabolism.

Adequate amounts of zinc are lacking in almost every common grain and forage. Although the minimum requirement for zinc is believed to be between 40 - 50 PPM in the total diet, the optimum range is probably closer to 90 PPM. But most common feeds contain levels below 40 PPM.

Typical Zinc Content of Common Forages and Grains

Alfalfa Hay	28 PPM	Corn	19 PPM
Bromegrass Hay	26 PPM	Oats	35 PPM
Orchardgrass Hay	36 PPM	Barley	17 PPM
Timothy Hay	38 PPM		

Interestingly, zinc deficiency is not a common problem, probably because most feed mills include some form of supplemental zinc in their grain rations. Inorganic sources of supplemental zinc include zinc oxide and zinc sulfate. Of these, zince sulfate is the most easily absorbed by the horse. Zinc is also available in polysaccharide and amino acid complexes, amino acid chelates, and proteinates.

The absorption rate of zinc is in the 10% - 15% range, and this rate can vary, according to how much zinc is already in the body, and the form in which zinc is supplied. Foals deficient in zinc will have poor appetites, a reduced rate of growth, hair loss, and dry, scaly skin.

Zinc is also needed for the growth and maintenance of the hoof wall, and for that reason it is widely used in hoof supplements, often in the form of zinc methionine complex. These supplements vary widely in their formulations, but the efficacy of some of the better ones cannot be denied.

High levels of zinc are well tolerated by horses, although too much of it can interfere with the utilization of other minerals, especially copper.

Selenium (Se)

In the case of selenium, if a little is good a lot is definitely not better. In fact, selenium is so toxic that, until the late 1970's, selenium could not legally be added to feed. Fortunately for horsemen, the FDA now permits the addition of selenium to horse feeds, a fact which makes life much easier for those living in areas of selenium deficient soils.

Along with vitamin E (a vitamin that works synergistically with selenium), selenium is needed for proper muscle development. It is a component of enzymes that detoxify peroxides that are toxic to cell membranes.

The maintenance requirement for selenium is estimated to be 0.1 PPM in the diet, while the maximum tolerable amount is 2 PPM in the total diet, or 20 times the maintenance requirement. Most feedstuffs contain between 0.05 - 0.3 PPM, though levels vary greatly, depending upon the nature of the soil. Areas low in selenium include the Great Lakes states, New England, Florida, northern California, western Oregon and western and northern Washington state. States that have localized areas with toxic levels of selenium include the band of states stretching from northern New Mexico and Texas through Montana and North Dakota.

A selenium deficiency in the foal manifests itself as white muscle disease, a form of muscular dystrophy, so called because the animal becomes pale in appearance. Symptoms include general weakness and labored movement, difficulty in nursing and swallowing, and irregular, labored breathing.

Acute selenium toxicity is sometimes called blind staggers, or simply alkali disease. Affected horses appear colicky with an elevated heart rate and irregular breathing. Horses appear to be blind. They can be seen pressing their heads against stationary objects, and may sweat profusely. These symptoms can be triggered by the ingestion of 150 milligrams per 100 lbs. of body weight, or 1.66 grams for an 1100 pound horse.

Symptoms of chronic toxicity include anemia, lameness and joint stiffness, a rough hair coat with loss of hair in the mane and tail, and malformed hooves with cracks around the coronary band. If these symptoms go unchecked for a long period time, chronic toxicity can cause death.

Selenium is easily absorbed by the body of the horse, with an efficiency rate above 75%. In nature selenium forms complexes with the amino acids cystine, cysteine, and methionine. Sodium selenite and sodium selenate are the usual supplemental forms.

Your goal in supplementing selenium should be to bring the selenium concentration in the entire ration to 0.1 PPM. Before supplementing, therefore, you should know how much you are already feeding. If you know where your hay was grown, a quick call to your county extension agent should be helpful in determining if it was grown in a selenium deficient area, or not. If in doubt have your hay tested; selenium is serious business.

Quick Summary of Trace Minerals

- **Trace minerals** are less abundant in soil than macrominerals.
- **Trace minerals** are diminishing from the soil, due mainly to the effects of farming.
- Organic forms of **copper, cobalt, iodine, iron, manganese** and **zinc** are absorbed better than inorganic forms.
- **Polysaccharide complexes** are sulfates enclosed in a polysaccharide coating.
- **Chelates** and **proteinates** are chemically bound to organic substrates, and are very effective.
- **Cobalt** is the central atom in the vitamin B_{12} molecule, which is needed for the formation of hemoglobin.
- **Copper** is part of several enzyme systems that maintain and synthesize connective tissue, aid in reproduction, and promote an active immune system.
- **Iodine** is used in the manufacture of thyroid hormones. A deficiency can cause goiters in young animals. Iodized salt will provide a horse with sufficient iodine.
- **Iron** is a constituent of hemoglobin and myoglobin, which transport and store oxygen in the blood and muscles.
- **Manganese** is needed by the enzymes that regulate the manufacture and utilization of chondroitin sulfates, important compounds in connective tissues.
- **Zinc** is part of several enzyme systems necessary for the growth and maintenance of hooves, hair and skin. It is lacking in almost every common feed.
- **Selenium** is needed for proper muscle growth and function. Soils in many areas of the U.S. are deficient, others contain toxic levels.

CHART OF DAILY MINERAL REQUIREMENTS

(Based on 1100 lb. Adult Weight)

	Calcium (g)	Phosphorus (g)	Magnesium (g)	Sulfur* (g)	Potassium (g)	Sodium** (g)	Cobalt* (mg)	Copper (mg)	Iodine (mg)	Iron (mg)	Manganese* (mg)	Zinc (mg)	Selenium (mg)
Pregnant Mare, Early to Mid	22	14	8.0	12.3	25	8.2	0.8	82	0.8	327	327	327	0.8
Pregnant Mare, 3rd Trimester	38	28	9.4	12.3	31	8.2	0.8	82	0.8	409	327	327	0.8
Lactating Mare	56	36	10.9	16.3	46	10.9	1.1	108	1.1	543	434	434	1.1
Foal at 3 months	35	20	4.0	8.2	12	5.5	0.5	65	0.5	275	220	230	0.5
Weanling at 6 months	38	21	4.7	10.2	15	6.8	0.7	145	0.7	380	275	375	0.7
Yearling at 12 months	39	22	7.5	15.9	25	10.6	1.1	150	1.1	530	400	400	1.1
Growing Horse at 18 months	40	23	8.6	16.1	28	10.7	1.1	150	1.1	536	429	430	1.1
Maintenance Horse	22	14	8.0	12.3	25	8.2	0.8	82	0.8	327	327	327	0.8
Performance Horse in Training	40	28.5	15.1	17.2	50	34.5	1.1	115	1.1	459	459	459	1.1
Breeding Stallion	25	17.8	9.4	12.8	31	8.5	0.9	85.3	0.9	341	341	341	0.9

* There is no minimum requirement established for this mineral. The quantities shown are based on NRC estimates for safe and adequate amounts.
** Salt is 39% Sodium.

Chapter 10

Vitamins

Every nutrient we have looked at so far has had some compelling chemical characteristic that makes it easy to identify a member of a specific group: carbohydrates contain hydrogen and oxygen in the same ratio as water; fats are all soluble in ether; proteins are made up of distinct amino acids, and minerals are simply individual elements put to work within the body as constituents of enzymes or other important compounds.

But vitamins have no distinctive chemical signature; some are readily soluble, others are not; some are alcohols, some more closely resemble proteins; some can take great extremes of heat, others fall apart at the slightest provocation; most, but not all, act as coenzymes, or parts of coenzymes. A chemist cannot look at a vitamin and declare it to be one, until it is proven empirically to be needed by the body.

So what is a vitamin? A vitamin is, by simple default, what is still needed by the body after it is given all the carbohydrates, fats, proteins and minerals it needs. Vitamins comprise the seemingly unlikely group of nutrients that fall through the nutritional cracks. To put it another way, if you were given a jigsaw puzzle called "The Nutritional Requirements of the Horse", and you arranged all the pieces of carbohydrates, fats, proteins, and minerals in proper order, you would see large gaps between the pieces. The gaps would be filled with vitamins, the mortar in the puzzle of nutrition.

Vitamins are classified as either fat-soluble or water-soluble, although this is not an absolute division, as some fat-soluble vitamins can be made to dissolve in water, and vice versa. The fat-soluble vitamins are vitamins only for vertebrates, while most of the water-soluble vitamins are needed by all animals. Most, but not all, water-soluble vitamins are present in yeast.

FAT-SOLUBLE VITAMINS

Vitamins A, D, E and K are the fat-soluble vitamins. All are guaranteed in IU (International Units) per pound, except for vitamin K which, along with the water-soluble vitamins, is guaranteed in milligrams per pound. Vitamin D_3 is sometimes guaranteed in ICU (International Chick Units), though IU is more common.

Vitamin A

The term "vitamin A" does not refer to any specific compound, but rather to a class of at least a dozen compounds that all display the same activity (i.e., of all-*trans*-retinol) in the body. Moreover, plants do not manufacture vitamin A; it is only made in the bodies of animals with backbones (and in large vitamin factories, mostly in Europe). What plants do make is a class of pigments known as the carotenoids, of which about 50 can—to varying degrees—be converted into vitamin A in the body. Of the carotenoids, the most important is beta carotene.

Vitamin A is important for vision, since it is a chief component of the light-sensitive pigment in the rods of the eye. It is also essential for cell differentiation (so bone cells become bone, and liver cells become liver), and to assist in the continuing process of bone remodeling in growing horses.

The list of symptoms that point toward a deficiency include:

poor growth and depressed appetite; progressive weakness; impaired reproductive function; continuously runny, teary eyes; night blindness; a hardening of the skin and the cornea of the eyes; respiratory infections, and abscesses of the salivary glands.

The NRC estimates the bare requirement for vitamin A to be 30 - 60 IU (International Units) per day, for each kilogram of body weight. For an 1100 pound horse this would translate to 15,000 - 30,000 IU per day. At the other end of the spectrum, the upper limit set by the NRC for vitamin A on a continual basis is 16,000 IU per kilogram of dry feed, which would be 160,000 IU for a horse weighing 1100 pounds and eating 22 pounds of dry matter per day. A safe bet would be to try for the middle ground—somewhere between 60,000-100,000 IU per day for an 1100 pound horse.

A horse on green pasture will get all the vitamin A it needs, precluding the need for any supplementation. But—since sunlight, moisture and time, itself, are anathema to beta carotene—fresh, green pasture contains 10 to 120 times more vitamin A than dried hay. And cereal grains, with the exception of corn, contain almost no beta carotene, so you should expect virtually all of your horse's vitamin A to come from forages and supplements.

But nature has a way of preparing for lean times. Vitamin A is stored well in the body, primarily in the liver, and beta carotene can be stored in fat cells within the body, where it can be converted into vitamin A as the need arises. Therefore, a horse taken off of green pasture and put on dried forages is a long way from developing a vitamin A deficiency.

Generally, stored hays contain less than 40 mgs./kg. of beta carotene. Now, since it is estimated that a horse can convert one milligram of beta carotene into 400 IU of vitamin A, a horse eating 8 kilograms (17.6 pounds) of hay per day will get only 3200 IU of vitamin A in its hay, at best, and perhaps a lot less. Fortunately, most feed mills add vitamin A to their grain mixes. The sweet feed

I use has 4000 IU per pound, so when I feed four pounds a day I am getting the bare minimum requirement for vitamin A. In the wintertime, or when I take a horse off of pasture, I also feed two ounces of a supplement that supplies 400,000 IU of vitamin A per pound (or 25,000 IU per ounce), which adds another 50,000 IU to the diet. This keeps an 1100 pound horse well within the comfort zone.

From Hay	3,200 IU
From Sweet Feed	16,000 IU
From Supplement	50,000 IU
Total Vitamin A	**69,200 IU**

Like almost anything else, too much vitamin A can be toxic. Signs of chronic toxicity include: abnormal thickening of the bone accompanied by bone fragility; flaky skin; poor muscle tone; rough haircoats and loss of hair; and depression. Mares fed toxic levels of vitamin A throughout their pregnancies can give birth to grotesquely disfigured foals. It's food for thought.

Many horsemen prefer to supplement with beta carotene, instead of vitamin A. Since beta carotene is the horse's natural source of vitamin A, it is hard to argue with that decision. Beta carotene is not toxic, and may have advantages over synthetic vitamin A, such as better reproductive performance in breeding stock, and antioxidant activity in performance horses. Unfortunately, it is quite expensive and not readily available in most feed and tack stores.

Vitamin D

Vitamin D is a most interesting vitamin; not because it possesses the ability to take a nag from the glue factory to the winner's circle, but because it is the only nutrient known that is more prevalent in dried forages, than in green pasture. This is because vitamin D_2 is made in plant tissues from the compound ergosterol, and ultraviolet light from the sun. But since active chlorophyll blocks the UV light from the underlying ergosterol, the vitamin D is produced only after the plant has been cut.

Fortunately for those of us who pasture our horses, another form of vitamin D (vitamin D_3) is made under the horse's skin from a form of cholesterol (7-dehydrocholesterol, to be precise), when the horse is exposed to sunlight. This all works out quite well, since the only horse liable to be denied access to sunlight is a stable-bound horse being fed dried forage.

By whatever means a horse gets its vitamin D, it is critically important that it does, because without vitamin D a life-threatening mineral imbalance will result. Vitamin D is part of the proteins that bind calcium and magnesium, facilitating their absorption. It also helps regulate the excretion of phosphates in the urine. Simply put, a vitamin D deficiency manifests itself as a deficiency of calcium, magnesium, and phosphorus.

Though a deficiency of vitamin D is extremely rare, when it does occur it produces rickets-like symptoms, including poor bone density, swollen joints, and a painful, labored gait.

An excess of vitamin D will result in the deposition of calcium in the soft tissues, primarily in the blood vessels, heart, lungs and kidneys. The most likely way for this to occur would be by the overfeeding of supplements containing vitamin D. Some plants, such as jasmine (Cestrum diurnum) contain a substance that causes hyper-absorption of calcium, and horses eating these plants can develop a condition that resembles vitamin D toxicity.

Although vitamin D supplementation is not considered necessary, especially for horses exposed to sunlight, the addition of vitamin D_3 to the feed of young growing horses, lactating mares, or mares in the final trimester of pregnancy may be helpful. The maximum safe level suggested by the NRC for feeding on a daily basis is 2,200 IU of vitamin D_3, per kilogram of dry matter in the diet. There are many supplements offered by reputable manufacturers that have safe levels of vitamin D_3.

Vitamin E

Of all the nutrients, vitamin E is the most altruistic. It selflessly offers itself up for annihilation, so that the body does not destroy itself. How does it do this? Well, it all has to do with oxygen, which can be very destructive at times. (I am painfully reminded of this fact every time I look at the rusted-out quarter panels on my old Chevy flatbed.) Vitamin E is easily oxidized, which is to say that it readily reacts with charged oxygen-containing compounds, thus preventing them from reacting with—and thereby destroying—fats and proteins in the cell membrane. Simply put, Vitamin E is the cell's cannon fodder in its interminable battle with free radicals.

The mineral selenium works with Vitamin E to protect cardiac and skeletal muscle tissues. Selenium is part of an enzyme that works to protect the interior of the cell, while vitamin E protects the outer portions of the cell.

Vitamin E is a common term applied to the substance tocopherol (pronounced "toe-KOF-er-all"), of which there are at least 8 known variants. The word tocopherol comes from the Greek words *tokos* (childbirth), and *pherein* (to carry, or bear), while the *-ol* ending denotes that it is an alcohol. It was so named after it was discovered that vitamin E would allow female rats, being fed rancid fat, to carry their pups to term. While vitamin E will be guaranteed on a feed label in IU per pound, tocopherol is customarily referred to in milligrams. Fortunately, one milligram of tocopherol is equivalent to one IU of vitamin E activity, so the terms are interchangeable for all practical purposes.

As with most other nutrients, deficiencies of vitamin E are most evident in young, growing horses. Young horses deprived of vitamin E experience a rapid degeneration of cardiac and skeletal muscles. Noticeable symptoms include exaggerated, uncoordinated movement, especially in the hind limbs, and a "sprawled" stance.

While the NRC has set no minimum requirement for vitamin E, it suggests that all horses should receive at least 50 mg. of tocopherol per kilogram of dry feed, while pregnant and lactating mares, growing foals, and performance horses might do better with 80 mg./kg. of dry diet. Since most forages and grains contain less than 30 mg./kg. of tocopherol (and hay considerably less if it has been rained on), some degree of supplementation would be helpful for most horses.

Pregnant mares need vitamin E to maintain normal reproductive function, and lactating mares need an extra supply to pass on to their foals in their milk. Young, growing horses require extra vitamin E to help with normal muscle development. Performance horses should have additional vitamin E to maintain the integrity of muscles that are constantly bombarded with the harmful oxidative by-products of anaerobic respiration. And, although it has never been conclusively proven that vitamin E improves a stallion's libido, most stallion owners—myself included—would not dare weather a breeding season without it.

If we assume that the non-supplemental portion of a normal diet contains around 30 mgs./kg. of tocopherol, this would leave a deficit of 500 - 600 IU of vitamin E for the average broodmare, 250 - 300 IU per day for a 3 - 4 month-old foal, and 650 - 750 IU per day for a performance horse in heavy training. There is no shortage of vitamin E supplements on the market. Most contain 2000 IU per ounce, in the form of dl-alpha tocopherol acetate (a stable form of tocopherol). Many include trace amounts of selenium. The manufacturers of these supplements recommend feeding 2000 IU per day to stallions, broodmares and horses in training, and sales are brisk. Aside from the cost, there is certainly no harm in feeding that much tocopherol to horses and, according to many trainers and farm managers, the benefits far outweigh the costs.

How much vitamin E is too much? More than most people can afford to feed. While vitamin E toxicity has never been observed in horses, the NRC feels the upper safe limit to be 75 IU per kilogram of body weight per day, or 37,500 IU for an 1100 pound horse.

Vitamin K

Vitamin K is required for the normal clotting of blood. Since it is synthesized in adequate quantities by bacteria in the gut, it is not considered to be of dietary significance for the horse. Vitamin K_3, as menadione, is often present in small quantities in vitamin supplements, and especially in preparation for "bleeders" (race horses that bleed through the lungs due to the rupture of pulmonary capillaries), though its efficacy in those preparations remains to be seen. While oral menadione appears to be relatively non-toxic, injectable menadione given for hemorrage can cause acute kidney failure and death.

WATER-SOLUBLE VITAMINS

The water-soluble vitamins include thiamin (B_1), riboflavin (B_2), niacin, pantothenic acid, pyridoxine (B_6), folic acid, choline, vitamin B_{12}, ascorbic acid (vitamin C), and biotin.

Thiamin (B₁)

The importance of thiamin (also known as thiamine) was discovered in 1890, on the island of Java, where it was found that the symptoms of beriberi could be reversed by feeding unhusked rice to affected individuals who had previously been subsisting on polished rice. Thiamin was isolated some 30 years later, and was synthesized for the first time in 1936.

The need for thiamin is directly related to the caloric requirements of the horse. In the body thiamin is converted to thiamin pyrophosphate, a compound required for the metabolism of pyruvic acid. Pyruvic acid, in turn, is an essential link in the chain of reactions that leads to the utilization of carbohydrates and proteins. If metabolic thiamin is insufficient, the horse cannot derive sufficient energy from its diet.

Although some thiamin is synthesized by bacteria in the gut, it does not appear to be enough to meet the thiamin requirement of the horse, since a deficiency can be triggered by feeding a thiamin deficient diet.

Signs of deficiency include nervousness; dull haircoat; loss of appetite; weight loss; lack of coordination in the hind quarters; and slowed or irregular heartbeat. A deficiency can occur from feeding poor quality hay, or by the ingestion of certain plants known to make thiamin unavailable to the body. These plants include: horsetail, yellow star thistle and bracken fern.

The NRC suggests that 3 mg./kg of dry feed is sufficient for maintenance, growth and reproduction, while 5 mg./kg. may be needed for the performance horse. Common cereal grains contain concentrations of thiamin in the range of 3 - 6 mg./kg.; dried forages even less. Brewers yeast, on the other hand, is an excellent source of thiamin, as it contains 85 - 90 mg./kg. of thiamin. Unfortunately, brewers yeast is fed in such small quantities that it cannot contribute significant amounts of thiamin to the total ration.

While some degree of thiamin supplementation would probably be helpful for all horses, it is especially beneficial for performance horses. Thiamin can help restore the appetites of horses that have gone off their feed, and in many cases it can help alleviate the nervousness of stall-bound horses on high-energy rations.

Thiamin is usually included in small quantities in vitamin/ mineral supplements. There are also a number of thiamin supplements on the market which contain concentrations from 100 to 1000 milligrams per ounce. These supplements are safe (except to your pocketbook), as the maximum safe limit for thiamin is at least 1000 times the minimum requirement.

Riboflavin (B₂)

Riboflavin is present in a number of enzymes systems involved in converting feed into energy, which makes it essential to every cell in the body. A deficiency of riboflavin has never been produced in the horse, but in the rat it causes retarded growth, hair loss, dermatitis and reddening of the eyes.

Horses synthesize riboflavin in the large intestine, but not quite enough to meet their daily demands. A minimum of 2 mg./kg. of dry diet is required. Good quality hay should contain 5 - 10 mg./kg. of riboflavin, while most grains contain less than 2 mg./kg.

Riboflavin supplementation should not be a concern for most horses, although performance horses on high-calorie diets may utilize their feed more efficiently with a little extra riboflavin. There is really no point in feeding a lot of it, because it cannot be stored in the body to any extent, and whatever is not used is quickly excreted, via the normal pathways.

Niacin

Niacin is the common term applied to two substances—nicotinic acid and nicotinamide—both of which have equal vitamin activity. The name "niacin" was adopted to avoid confusion—or guilt by association—with the addictive alkaloid, nicotine. The nutritional significance of niacin was discovered in 1938, when it was found to be the nutritional factor lacking in the diets of dogs with "black tongue disease", and in people with pellagra. These conditions are characterized by loss of appetite, muscular weakness, digestive disorders, dermatitis and anemia.

Niacin is a part of a pair of enzymes that are critical in the metabolism of carbohydrates, fats, and amino acids. Some niacin is synthesized by microbes in the gut, from the amino acid tryptophan. Ample amounts can also be found in forages, protein sources, and in cereal grains, although most of the niacin in grains is bound in unusable forms.

There is no dietary requirement established for niacin, and no one has ever observed a niacin deficient horse. Just the same, niacin often finds its way into vitamin supplements, sometimes in relatively large amounts. Don't ask; I don't know.

Pantothenic Acid

Pantothenic acid is a component of coenzyme A, which is involved in energy metabolism. It is also essential for the synthesis of steroids, including cholesterol, and for the production of adrenal hormones. It is synthesized to some degree in the intestine, but a dietary source is also needed.

No one really knows the dietary requirement for pantothenic acid, since a deficiency has never been observed in the horse, but 15 PPM in the diet is generally considered adequate. Brewers yeast is an excellent source, with over 80 PPM. Good quality hay should contain at least 20 PPM, while cereal grains range from 5 - 10 PPM.

Pyridoxine (B₆)

Pyridoxine is another vitamin that is a component of enzyme systems involved in the metabolism of protein, fats and carbohydrates. It is also required for the formation of red blood cells. Pyridoxine is the form of vitamin B_6 found in plants. It is later converted in the body into pyridoxal and pyridoxamine.

Pyridoxine is synthesized by microflora in the gut, and it is found in small amounts in forages, grains, and protein sources. No minimum dietary requirement has been established for pyridoxine, as no deficiency of this vitamin has ever been observed in the horse. But since it is a component in the system that turns feed into energy, the need for it increases with the energy demands of the horse. For that reason, it is often added to supplements for performance horses and pregnant mares.

Folic Acid

It was recently discovered that the addition of folic acid to the diets of pregnant women would greatly reduce the incidence of certain forms of birth defects. The FDA was so impressed that they immediately issued a proclamation requiring flour manufacturers to add folic acid to the flour they produced for human consumption.

To find a meaningful correlation with horses may be difficult, however, since one of the richest sources of folic acid—grass—is a common feed for horses and a most uncommon one for humans. In fact, most of what a horse eats is richer in folic acid than most of what people eat (except for those of us who enjoy green, leafy vegetables), so the likelihood of a deficiency in horses—especially one leading to birth defects—is slight.

Folic acid has a number of functions in the body. It is needed for the formation of red blood cells, the synthesis of methionine, and the formation of nucleic acids.

While it is known that folic acid is synthesized by intestinal bacteria, it is not certain how much of a horse's daily requirements are met by this process. The dietary requirement has not been established for the horse, but since no signs of deficiency have ever been reported, a normal diet is thought to contain sufficient folic acid.

Just the same, folic acid is usually included in vitamin supplements, where it may be of some benefit to pregnant and lactating mares (who always need more of everything), and performance horses, since folic acid is lost in sweat, and because they manufacture more blood than most other horses.

Choline

Choline is a compound that is always included in discussions of water-soluble vitamins, albeit with some hesitancy. Unlike the other B vitamins, choline has no known catalytic role in the body, which is to say that it is not a part of any enzyme, or coenzyme. It is further set apart from other members of the group by the fact that it is synthesized in the liver, rather than in the intestine.

Although it may be different, choline is still vitally important. As a constituent of acetylcholine, it is needed for the transmission of nerve impulses from neuron to neuron. It acts in synergy with methionine as a methyl donor, where it has a role in fat metabolism. Choline is also a structural component of cell membranes.

For all of its many metabolic roles, no one has ever studied the horse's requirements for choline, just as no one has ever produced a choline deficient horse. The abundance of choline in forages and grains can easily make up for any shortfall in metabolic synthesis, making a deficiency highly improbable. Just the same, choline chloride (which is quite inexpensive) is added in liberal amounts to most vitamin supplements.

Vitamin B_{12} (Cobalamin)

Vitamin B_{12} is another vitamin that stands out among the water-soluble vitamins. Containing a single atom of cobalt in its core, it is not produced by any plants, even though plants take cobalt into their tissues. The only natural vitamin B_{12} is produced by microorganisms, many of which are found in the horse's intestines.

Vitamin B_{12} was the last vitamin to be discovered (1948) and, considering how little of it is needed, it is the most potent. And yet it shows no signs of toxicity in amounts several hundred times what is considered necessary.

It is essential for the production of red blood cells, and for this reason it is almost always included in vitamin supplements (usually in the form of cyanocobalamin) formulated for performance horses. Interestingly, these supplements also contain ample amounts of cobalt, just to cover all the bases, I would imagine.

Vitamin B_{12} can be stored indefinitely within the organs of the body, primarily in the liver, so horses deprived of cobalt, or horses suffering temporary depletion of intestinal microflora (from parasites or disease) can rely on their stores of B_{12} for weeks or months, if necessary. There is no evidence of a dietary need for vitamin B_{12}, beyond what is synthesized in the gut.

Ascorbic Acid

On food labeled for human consumption, ascorbic acid is referred to as "vitamin C"; on feed and supplements labeled for horses it must be guaranteed as "ascorbic acid". The difference arises not from a double standard for horses and humans, but from the fact that horses manufacture ascorbic acid in their livers, from glucose, while humans do not. For us, as well as other primates, ascorbic acid must be present in the diet. For humans, then, ascorbic acid is a vitamin; for horses it is simply a metabolic essential.

Ascorbic acid's most important role in the body is in its capacity as a cofactor in the synthesis of collagen, the most prevalent protein in the animal world. Collagen is, literally, the protein that holds us—and our horses—together. It is a primary constituent of connective tissues, including skin, tendons, bone and cartilage.

Ascorbic acid is added to a whole range of supplements, especially those formulated to help repair damaged cartilage, or in preparations for bleeders. While the fundamental logic of this is evident, in practice it is of little or no value. Why? Because ascorbic acid is very poorly absorbed by horses, probably because it is broken down by microflora before it ever gets to the bloodstream. It takes a dose of 20 grams or more to raise the level of ascorbic acid in the blood.

There is, therefore, no dietary requirement for ascorbic acid in the horse, as there appears to be no dietary pathway for its utilization.

Biotin

For over a decade, biotin has been at the center of a heated debate involving horsemen, feed manufacturers, various state agriculture officials, the FDA, and of course, the horse. The controversy over biotin is so intense that the FDA has, in some cases, quarantined biotin as an "unapproved animal drug". While this may appear to be a cavalier move, the FDA is actually on solid legal footing, since according to the "Federal Food, Drug and Cosmetic Act", a substance is treated as a drug as soon as someone claims it has a drug-like effect, be it biotin or beef broth.

What could possibly be so controversial about a B-complex vitamin? Well, it all began in the late 1970's, when a feed mill proprietor and a veterinarian in Britain decided to add 10 - 15 milligrams of biotin per day to the rations of certain horses under the veterinarian's care, to see if it could help the unacceptably poor condition of their hooves. After 5 months of biotin supplementation, the condition of all the affected hooves had, in fact, improved dramatically.

This was big news, and once it got out, the supplement manufacturers were climbing over the top of each other to be the first on the market with a biotin supplement. New companies sprang up overnight. Promotional literature and advertisements making miraculous claims for the effect this vitamin could have on hoof quality soon followed. All the hype immediately hit a vulnerable spot with the horse-keeping public; after all, a horse's hoof is like a person's hair: no matter how good it looks, it can always look better.

Meanwhile, the FDA was frantically reading and clipping all of these sensational ads and adding them to the dossiers it keeps on each of the supplement manufacturers. By the definitions set forth in the "Federal Food, Drug, and Cosmetic Act", the manufacturers were making "drug claims", even though most of the ads clearly stated that biotin was a vitamin. Once the FDA had seen enough, it mobilized its army of agents, who began paying friendly visits to the supplement manufacturers. Ads were pulled, literature was seized, and products with suggestive names were removed from the market. The battle lines were drawn.

The problem for the FDA was (and is) that biotin is a vitamin, and vitamins fall outside of its jurisdiction. As long as the supplement manufacturers do not claim that biotin can do things the FDA is not convinced it does, they are free from bureaucratic entanglements. This was really no problem for the manufacturers, because any copywriter worth her or his salt can lead you to believe that a given substance can do anything, without actually claiming that it has any effect, whatsoever. I know this to be true, because I used to be one of those copywriters.

But the fire of controversy has, for the most part, burned itself out, though certain state agricultural officials still hold a grudge of such enduring dimensions that they steadfastly refuse to believe that supplemental biotin is of any help to the horse, no matter what evidence to the contrary is put in front of them.

All that being said, can biotin help a horse with bad feet? In most cases the answer is yes, although the people doing the research are hard-pressed to explain how, or why. Biotin, like several other B-vitamins, is an integral part of a number of enzymes involved in the synthesis of glucose, fats, proteins, and even RNA and DNA. A horse, or a horseman, could not live long without it. Most plants contain small amounts of biotin, though most of it is bound to proteins that inhibit absorption in the gut. Fortunately biotin is synthesized in the intestine to such an extent that a biotin deficiency has never been described in the horse. Even horses with pathologically bad feet have blood biotin concentrations comparable to those horses with good feet, making it doubtful that weak, crumbly hooves are caused by a simple deficiency of biotin.

Nonetheless, in study after study, horses with poor hooves have responded to treatment with biotin, supplemented in amounts ranging from 10 to 20 milligrams per day. Treatment periods for these various trials have ranged from 5 months to 2 years, and often the hooves of the treated horses return to their original weak, thin-walled condition after supplemental biotin is removed from the diet.

What is going on here? It has been suggested that biotin might help inhibit the premature decay of the horn cells comprising the outer wall of the hoof. This would keep the wall strong and pliable while new horn is laid down in an environment much more conducive to growth. But this does not explain why horses with bad feet have as much biotin in their blood as horses with good feet. There may be other nutrients involved, the need for which might be compensated for by an abundance of biotin. It may be related to the single atom of sulfur in the biotin molecule, since sulfur is vitally important to the health of the hoof.

No one knows for certain, but odds are that a horse on good feed that still has bad feet can be helped with supplemental biotin.

Quick Summary of Vitamins

- **Vitamins** are nutrients needed by the body, though they do not fit into the categories of carbohydrates, fats, proteins, or minerals.
- **Vitamin A** is needed for vision, cell differentiation, and the remodeling of bone. It is manufactured in the body from carotenoids. **Vitamin A (as beta carotene)** is abundant in fresh, green forages, but generally lacking in other feeds.
- **Vitamin D_2** is more abundant in dried forages than fresh ones.
- **Vitamin D_3** is manufactured under the skin in the presence of sunlight.

continued on next page

- **Vitamin D** regulates the absorption of calcium and magnesium, and the excretion of phosphorus. A **vitamin D** deficiency manifests itself as a deficiency of these minerals.
- **Vitamin E** is needed for normal muscle development and reproductive function. As an antioxidant, it protect muscles cells from the oxidative by-products of anaerobic respiration.
- Broodmares, growing foals, breeding stallions and performance horses should all receive some supplemental **vitamin E**.
- **Vitamin K** is needed for the normal clotting of blood. Intestinal bacteria synthesize sufficient **vitamin K** for most horses.
- **Thiamin** and **riboflavin** are both necessary for energy metabolism. Supplemental **thiamin** is beneficial to horses on high carbohydrate diets.
- A deficiency of **riboflavin** has never been produced in the horse, but horses with high energy demands may be helped with the addition of **riboflavin** to the diet.
- **Niacin** is part of two enzymes necessary for carbohydrate, fat and protein metabolism. A deficiency has never been observed, or created, in the horse.
- **Pantothenic acid** is a component of an enzyme involved in energy metabolism, synthesis of steroids and adrenal hormones.
- **Folic Acid** is needed for the formation of red blood cells, the synthesis of methionine, and the formation of nucleic acids.
- **Choline** is necessary for the transmission of nerve impulses, and as a methyl donor in fat metabolism.
- **Vitamin B$_{12}$** is essential for the production of red blood cells. It is manufactured in the gut in the presence of cobalt.
- **Ascorbic acid** is manufactured in the horse's liver from the blood sugar, glucose. Its most important function in the body is in the synthesis of the connective protein, collagen.
- Dietary **ascorbic acid** appears to be of little benefit, since it is very poorly absorbed.
- **Biotin** is part of several enzymes involved in the synthesis of glucose, fats, proteins, and nucleic acids.
- **Biotin** has been shown to help horses with poor-quality hooves, though the reason for it remains elusive.

Vitamins

Chapter 11

A GUIDE TO
SUPPLEMENTAL
FEEDING

We have covered over 30 nutrients in the preceding pages, and I have offered suggestions for when it would be most appropriate to include these nutrients in the rations of the various classes of horses. But unless you have a far more tenacious memory than I, you will probably find yourself flipping back and forth between pages to keep it all straight in your mind. This makes for dog-eared books and frustrated readers. So, to keep this book—and your patience—intact, I have put together the following 2-page chart as a guide to supplemental feeding, the operative word here being "guide". It is *not* designed to cover every horse, in every situation. No chart could ever do that. It *is* an easy reference to use when considering the applicability of feeds and supplements to your feeding program.

It is not within the chart's parameters to address the needs of horses suffering from disease, injury or other pathological conditions, such as heavy parasite loads, or nutrient imbalances caused by improper feeding or peculiar soil conditions. For instance, when it is suggested that biotin supplementation is probably not critical, it should not be construed to mean that biotin is not an effective means to improve the condition of poor-quality hooves. By the same token, an anemic horse may well be helped by the addition of vitamin B_{12} to the diet, even though the chart shows that supplementation is of little or no value. Conversely, if you live in an area with high iodine concentrations in the soil, you do not need to supplement iodine, no matter what the chart indicates.

I have not included carbohydrates here, since they are the basis of all natural feeds. Nor have I included the "exotic nutrients", MSM, DMG and chondroitin sulfates; the use of these nutrients is purely a matter of choice by the individual horseman in consideration of each individual horse.

And remember: even though we horsemen are in independent lot who like to work things out on our own, it never hurts to seek the advise of a good nutritionist or veterinarian, or a reputable feed company when formulating rations.

GUIDE TO SUPPLEMENTAL FEEDING
PART I

	Maintenance Horse or Early Pregnancy	Late Pregnancy	Lactating Mare	Growing Horse	Performance Horse	Breeding Stallion
Protein	★	❖	◆	◆	❖	❖
Fat	★	★	★	★	❖	★
MINERALS						
Calcium	✪	❖	❖	❖	❖	✪
Phosphorus	✪	❖	❖	❖	❖	✪
Magnesium	★	★	★	★	❖	★
Sulfur	★	★	★	★	★	★
Potassium	✪	✪	✪	✪	◆	✪
Salt	◆	◆	◆	◆	◆	◆
Cobalt	★	★	★	★	★	★
Copper	★	❖	❖	◆	❖	❖
Iodine	◆	◆	◆	◆	◆	◆
Iron	★	★	★	★	★	★
Manganese	✪	❖	❖	◆	◆	❖
Zinc	◆	◆	◆	◆	◆	◆
Selenium	✪	✪	✪	✪	✪	✪

continued on next page

◆   Should definitely supplement, except under extrordinary conditions.

❖   Should probably supplement.

★   May be supplemented, but probably not critical.

✪   Supplementation depends on amount present in feeds.

○   Should not supplement, or supplementation is of little or no value.

GUIDE TO SUPPLEMENTAL FEEDING

PART 2

VITAMINS	Maintenance Horse or Early Pregnancy	Late Pregnancy	Lactating Mare	Growing Horse	Performance Horse	Breeding Stallion
Vitamin A	❖	❖	❖	❖	❖	❖
Vitamin D	★	❖	❖	❖	★	★
Vitamin E	★	◆	◆	◆	◆	◆
Vitamin K	○	○	○	○	○	○
Thiamin	★	❖	❖	❖	◆	❖
Riboflavin	★	★	★	★	❖	★
Niacin	★	★	★	★	★	★
Pantothenic Acid	★	★	★	★	❖	★
Pyridoxine	★	❖	❖	★	❖	★
Folic Acid	★	★	★	★	❖	★
Choline	★	★	★	★	★	★
Vitamin B_{12}	○	○	○	○	○	○
Ascorbic Acid	○	○	○	○	○	○

◆   *Should definitely supplement except under extrordinary conditions.*

❖   *Should probably supplement.*

★   *May be supplemented, but probably not critical.*

✪   *Supplementation depends on amount present in feeds.*

○   *Should not supplement, or supplementation is of little or no value.*

Chapter 12

EXOTIC NUTRIENTS

I f you never fed your horse anything other than the nutrients we have discussed up to this point, your horse would probably live a long and healthy life. This is not to say that we have covered every nutrient known. Chromium, silicon, nickel and fluorine are among the other nutrients—all needed by the horse in very small quantities—that are adequately supplied by natural feeds. There are thousands of compounds in feed that the body can make use of, and each of these could rightly be called a nutrient.

But there are certain nutrients on the market these days—politically hot nutrients—that are racking up millions of dollars in sales each year. If you live in certain states (Texas comes to mind) these nutrients are controlled as strictly as cocaine, and subject to seizure.

The three nutrients discussed here—MSM, DMG (dimethylglycine), and chondroitin sulfates—all occur naturally, either within the horse's tissues or in its natural feedstuffs. All are expensive nutrients administered in small quantities, and all are things the FDA wishes it had never heard of. They are big ticket items in the feed room, and yet horsemen are lined up to buy them. I do not advocate the use of any of these nutrients, but neither do I feel their use to be unwarranted. None has shown any toxic properties when used according to the manufacturer's instructions. It has been my experience that horsemen are among the least gullible people on the planet, and I have no doubt that those of us with good horses and thin pocketbooks would not be shelling out money, again and again, to buy things of no value. If you have performance horses, you have probably lost competitions to horses being fed these nutrients. On the other hand, you have probably won against others, who relied on these nutrients at the expense of good protein and sufficient carbohydrates. There are a hundred ways to win any game, but if the basics are forgotten, what remains is a hundred ways to lose.

MSM (DIMETHYL SULFONE)

If I had one-tenth of the money paid to the lawyers who have haggled over the rights to this diminutive molecule, I would probably be writing this book from the porch of a cabin on Isla de las Mujeres, in the Gulf of Mexico, rather than my home in dry and dusty eastern Colorado. Although MSM is a naturally occurring compound, its use in animal feeds (and human foods) is covered under several fiercely defended patents that have endured every challenge against them, to date. The FDA got into the fray several years ago when it brought suit against a prominent supplier of MSM in an abortive attempt to have the substance classified as a food additive, rather than a food. Under this classification, it would fall under the FDA's jurisdiction, and could be removed from the market-place at its whim. Much to the FDA's chagrin, it was proven in that case that MSM was, indeed, a natural compound (a food) that is ubiquitous in the plant and animal kingdoms, and therefore it could not be classified as a food additive.

MSM is an acronym for methylsulfonylmethane, also known as dimethyl sulfone. Structurally, it is as elegant as it is simple. It is composed of a central sulfur atom straddled between two methyl

(CH$_3$) groups, and two oxygen atoms. It is manufactured from DMSO (dimethyl sulfoxide), a by-product of paper manufacture, by treating DMSO with hydrogen peroxide in a potentially explosive reaction that yields MSM and water.

Nutritionally, MSM has two things going for it: like the amino acid, methionine, and the vitamin, choline, MSM is a methyl donor, which makes it a player in fat and energy metabolism. Also, MSM is an excellent source of metabolically available sulfur, a fact of no small significance. At present it is believed by most authorities that methionine is the body's most important source of dietary sulfur, but it is wasteful and inefficient for the body to tear protein apart to free up sulfur.

The importance of sulfur in the body is well known, though the requirements for it are not. As noted earlier, sulfur is present in the vitamins biotin and thiamin, the amino acids methionine and cystine, and in chondroitin sulfates. Sulfur gives shape and structural support to virtually all the tissues of the body.

MSM is abundant in fresh green forages (but not dried hay) and in mare's milk. (Curiously, it is also found in coffee, tea, and beer.) That it is a normal constituent of the equine diet is not in dispute. Neither is the fact that MSM is an excellent source of dietary sulfur. The nagging question is, what mode of action could MSM have in the body to account for the broad range of conditions it is reputed to treat? Is it simply from the free sulfur it provides, or is there something else? Neither of these questions has ever been adequately answered.

The conditions to which MSM has been applied are legion, and I have no intention of listing them all, but a few of the more important applications deserve mention. MSM has been used successfully (though not in controlled studies) to help, or cure: epiphysitis; navicular disease; arthritis; pulmonary hemorrhage (bleeders syndrome); dull hair coat; and dry, brittle hooves. The reports are both anecdotal accounts from individual horsemen and veterinarians, and research findings from trained investigators.

Is MSM a useful nutrient? Yes, though it is probably not the panacea that so many over-zealous marketing people claim it is. If you feed it, feed it for the sulfur, and a world of good things can come from that, alone.

DMG (DIMETHYLGLYCINE)

DMG—known to chemists as N, N-dimethylglycine—has been called a vitamin (vitamin B_{15}) by some researchers; pangamic acid by the Russians; a food additive and a drug by the FDA (who has had no luck in getting the courts to follow either line of reasoning); and a food, by those companies who market it.

Whatever you call it, DMG is a natural compound in food and feed, and animal tissues. Its metabolic roles have been well researched, although the resulting physiological implications are still being fleshed out. Probably of most interest to horsemen is the way in which DMG assists in the process of aerobic respiration. It appears to aid in the transport of oxygen across the cell to the mitochondria, small organelles within the cell where energy reactions take place. By making more oxygen available for aerobic respiration, DMG delays the buildup of lactic acid in the muscles. It also helps in the breakdown of lactic acid in the muscles and the blood. Since lactic acid is a limiting factor in the quality of a performance—and the recovery time following the performance—any nutrient that enhances respiration is potentially beneficial.

DMG has been on the market since the 1970's, and has been used safely by thousands of human and equine athletes.

Chondroitin Sulfates

Connective tissue, particularly joint cartilage, is composed primarily of three substances: water, collagens (proteins that are the basic building blocks of connective tissues), and proteoglycans, which are long chains of glycosaminoglycans (GAG's) in a protein matrix. Among the GAG's, those most widely distributed throughout the body are chondroitin sulfates.

Chondroitin sulfates are not a natural part of the equine diet. Although they do occur in some plants, they are tightly bound to other compounds that inhibits their digestion. Rather, they are synthesized within the connective tissue by specialized cells called chondrocytes. Dietary chondroitin sulfates are usually purified from bovine trachea, although they can be found in shark cartilage and in the green-lipped mussel, a mollusk harvested off the coast of New Zealand.

The rationale for feeding something to a horse that is not a natural part of its diet is simple: since we ask horses to do things they do not naturally do, then we may have to feed them things they do not naturally eat. No horse left on its own would beat itself up as badly as a race horse gets beat up. The extra, unnatural stresses put on the joint cartilage can easily break it down at a faster rate than the body can repair it.

Studies show that dietary chondroitin sulfates are at least 40% absorbed by the horse. Besides adding to the inventory of cartilage repair material, they have been shown to stimulate the chondrocytes to produce their own GAG's, and to inhibit the production of enzymes destructive to joint tissues.

Chondroitin sulfates, then, could be a helpful addition to the diet of any horse whose joints take a hammering. There are a number of reputable manufacturers of chondroitin sulfate supplements, but be prepared to spend some money—they don't come cheap.

Chapter 13

CLOSING CONSIDERATIONS: THE BASICS, THE BASICS, THE BASICS

We have spent a good portion of this book discussing minerals and vitamins, because each one is unique and essential to the health of all horses. If any one of the non-energy nutrients were somehow denied a horse, the horse would eventually die. Fortunately, it is practically impossible to deprive a well-fed horse of enough of most of these nutrients to cause it mortal harm, since they are either present in natural feeds, or are manufactured in the body. But it is quite easy to deprive a horse of enough energy and protein, and the horseman who does will quickly run into trouble.

TEETH AND PARASITES

A horse with dental and/or parasite problems will show signs of energy and protein deprivation, no matter how well it is fed. Imagine trying to chew your food if just one molar on one side of your mouth were ¼ inch longer than all the others; all the grinding and chewing of food would be restricted to that tooth, and the one directly below it. Although this usually doesn't happen to people, it is a common occurrence with horses. Horses teeth are slowly pushed out of their sockets throughout life. This is why the teeth of an older horse appear longer than those of younger horses, even though the teeth stop growing at the age of five. The process of the teeth retreating from their bony anchors is not always uniform, and an older horse can often end up with one or more teeth protruding farther than the others. When this happens, the teeth need to be "floated", a term which is dreamy euphemism for "ground, chipped, and broken-off with the Mother of all rasps". They can also be clipped off with nips designed specifically for that purpose. But as painful as this sounds, it actually causes the horse no discomfort beyond that of having its mouth pried open and its tongue held by the vet, since horses do not have nerves in their teeth. A horse that slobbers its food is a prime candidate for having its teeth checked, as is any horse that is a bad keeper.

Parasites, both internal and external, are probably the major cause of unthriftiness in well-fed horses. They range from single-celled organisms, to worms and mites (which are close relatives of spiders), and the one thing they all have in common is that they draw their nourishment from the body of your horse. No area of the country is free of parasites, though as a general rule they are more prevalent in the warmer, southern states. There are a number of good preparations on the market for ridding a horse of parasites. Your veterinarian would be the person to consult for advice on which products to use in your area, and how often they should be used.

FORAGES

I have spoken at length about forages throughout this book, and have given average analyses for a number of the nutrients they each contain. More consideration has been paid to dried hays, rather than pastures, because most horses depend on hays for roughage. The hays used in the examples —alfalfa, bromegrass, orchardgrass and timothy—are a good representation of the hays commonly fed to horses. Alfalfa is a legume, which means that it fixes atmospheric nitrogen in nodules in its roots. In essence, legumes possess the ability to fertilize themselves. Other legumes used for forage include red clover and birdsfoot trefoil, both of which are similar in composition to alfalfa. All of the hays used as examples also make excellent pastures. As pastures, they are all high in nutrients, though their moisture content may prevent a horse from consuming enough to meet its energy needs. So even with green, lush, pasture, supplemental feed should be a consideration. Other pasture grasses, such as Bermudagrass or Bahiagrass, grown primarily in the southern states, are less digestible than northern grasses.

Most horses will eat between 1% and 2% of their body weight in dry forages every day. For those of us who rely on baled hay, this means that we have to procure two to four tons of hay each year for every horse we own, a fact that underscores the importance of finding good hay. The way in which hay is put up can have at least as great an effect on its nutrient value as the soil on which the hay is grown. Hay that was rained on will have far less nutritional value than hay that was baled without rain. Overly dry hay will likewise be less nutritious than hay that was baled with adequate moisture, and the dust it puts off may cause respiratory problems, such as heaves, in some horses. When examining hay, look for a rich, green color inside the bale, a pliability to the leaves, and an absence of mold and dust. Good hay put up badly is worse than poor hay put up right.

If you are feeding hay that you are not familiar with, it is advisable to have it tested for digestible energy, crude protein, calcium and phosphorus, and any other nutrient you have concerns about. Even though hay may look good, it might be deficient in nutrients.

A word of caution about grass clippings: it is really not a good idea to feed your horse grass clippings from your lawn, unless you spread them out over a large area where the horse will have to spend hours picking them up. Although it is certainly a natural feed for horses, it is too much of a good thing. Its rapid fermentation in the gut can induce a life-threatening case of gas colic.

GRAINS, FATS, AND EXTRA PROTEIN

Cereal grains are energy feeds. Pound for pound, they supply about half-again as much energy as hays. Of the three grains discussed throughout this book, corn is the highest in digestible energy, followed by barley, and then oats. All three grains generally have protein values between 7.5% and 12% (with corn at the low end), making them comparable in protein to average hays.

Oats, corn and barley, either alone or in combination, make excellent feed for horses. They are the feed of first resort when more energy is needed in the diet. Knowing the caloric needs of the different classes of horses is of primary importance, since everything that goes on within the horse requires energy.

As noted earlier, fat is also an excellent source of energy. Fat should be a consideration for any horse with high caloric demands, such as race horses, where a source of more concentrated energy is needed to cut down on the sheer bulk of feed. Vegetable oils, particularly corn oil, are better sources of fat than animal fats; they are more palatable and are less likely to become rancid.

Some form of supplemental protein is beneficial to most horses, and critically important to others, such as growing horses and lactating mares. Besides the sources already mentioned (soybean, cottonseed and linseed meals), peanut meal, sunflower meal and dehydrated brewer's grains (malt pellets) are also used. Dried skimmed milk is a good source of animal protein; it is palatable to the horse and it is also high in lysine compared to vegetable proteins.

BASICS OF A SUCCESSFUL FEEDING PROGRAM

1. Good teeth
2. Absence of parasites
3. Good hay or pasture
4. Ample sources of energy
5. Sufficient sources of good protein

And, lest we forget:

6. Good water, free choice
7. Salt (preferably iodized), free choice

If all of the above are provided for your horse, your chances of having feeding related problems will be minimal. But if one or more of these seven items is overlooked, well.........
No, I don't need to say it.

Appendix

HELPFUL FORMULAS AND CONVERSION FACTORS

In preparing the tables for this book I had to use several different mathematical conversions to put the information into forms that were readily understandable. Many of them were intuitive, others were not. For those who do not work with these units on a daily basis, I will give a few formulas that should enable anyone to translate a feed label into easier terms, and thereby formulate their own rations.

Feed labels are a marriage of metric and avoirdupois units, which is a mixed blessing. People who are familiar with the metric system find that it is logical and easy to use. Every unit is a power of ten above or below another unit. Units of volume are equivalent to units of liquid measure, such that a cubic centimeter is the same volume as a milliliter, which makes 1000 cc's equivalent to a liter. Furthermore, the metric system is based on the specific gravity of water at standard temperature and pressure, which means that one gram of water occupies one cc (or one ml) of space, and one liter (1000 cc's) of water weighs one kilogram. (By contrast, how many people know, as a matter of casual knowledge, how many cubic inches are in one gallon of water?)

This is all well and good, except that most of us were brought up thinking in ounces, pounds, feet, inches, pints, quarts, and gallons. Whenever we see grams, the brain asks for ounces. Unfortunately, ounces just do not work when dealing with small quantities, such as the amount of copper in a pound of sweet feed. It is much easier to say "18.5 milligrams" than "$1/1532^{nd}$ of an ounce".

Like it or not, the metric system is a fact of life when it comes to horse feeds, and the horseman who takes the time to become familiar with it will be miles (or kilometers) ahead of the neighbor down the road, who doesn't.

Helpful Conversions

One Pound = 16 ounces

One ounce = 28.35 grams

One pound = 453.6 grams

One pound = 453,600 milligrams

One pound = 0.45 kilograms

One gram = 1000 milligrams

One kilogram = 1000 grams

One kilogram = 2.2 pounds

Percent to Milligrams per Day

Percentages are used extensively in feed labeling. Protein, fat, fiber, calcium, phosphorus, magnesium and salt are always guaranteed in percentages, and often other minerals will be, too.

Question:

If you are feeding 4 pounds of a sweet feed that guarantees 0.012% zinc per pound, how many milligrams of zinc are you feeding per day?

Solution:

Step 1.   *Convert pounds to milligrams:*
4 lbs. x 453,600 mg./lb. = 1,814,400 milligrams

Step 2.   *Convert percentage to actual value (divide by 100, or simply move the decimal point 2 places to the left):*
0.012% ÷ 100 = .00012

Step 3.   *Multiply total milligrams by the number from Step 2:*
1,814,400 mgs. x .00012 = **217.728 mg. of zinc in 4 pounds of feed.**

Percent to Grams per Day

It works just the same with minerals like calcium, except that we use grams instead of milligrams.

Question:

How many grams of calcium are in 5 pounds of feed with a 0.6% calcium content?

Solution:

Step 1. *Convert pounds to grams:*
5 lbs. x 453.6 g./lb. = 2268 grams

Step 2. *Convert percentage to actual value (divide by 100, or simply move the decimal point 2 places to the left):*
0.6% ÷ 100 = .006

Step 3. *Multiply total grams by the number from Step 2:*
2268 g. x .006 = **13.608 grams of calcium in 5 pounds of feed.**

PPM to Milligrams per Day

Trace minerals, such as zinc, copper, iron, etc., should be guaranteed as PPM, or "parts per million".

Question:

If you are feeding your horse two ounces per day of a supplement that guarantees 8500 PPM of iron, how many milligrams of iron is the horse getting?

Solution:

Step 1. Convert ounces to grams:

2 ounces x 28.35 g./oz. = 56.7 grams

Step 2. Convert grams to milligrams (multiply by 1000, or simply move the decimal point 3 places to the left):

56.7 grams x 1000 = 56,700 milligrams

Step 3. Convert PPM to actual number (divide by 1,000,000 or simply move the decimal point 6 places to the left):

8500 PPM ÷ 1,000,000 = .008500 or .0085

Step 4. Multiply total milligrams by the number from Step 3:

56,700 mg. x .0085 = **481.95 milligrams of iron in 2 ounces of supplement.**

TOTAL PROTEIN IN A RATION

Question:

Let's say you are feeding 14 pounds of hay, that is 12.5% protein and 6 pounds of supplement that is 16% protein. What is the protein percentage of the entire ration?

Solution:

Step 1. *Find the protein factor for each feed:*

14 lbs. hay x 12.5% protein = 175

6 lbs. supplement x 16% protein = 96

Step 2. *Add the protein factors and the total pounds:*

175 + 96 = 271

14 lbs. + 6 lbs. = 20 lbs.

Step 3. *Divide total protein factor by total pounds:*

271 ÷ 20 lbs = **13.55% protein in the entire ration.**

Question:

How many grams of protein are in the ration listed above?

Solution (same as page 118):

Step 1. *Convert total pounds to grams:*

20 lbs. x 453.6 g./lb. = 9072 grams

Step 2. *Convert total percentage to actual value (divide by 100, or simply move the decimal point 2 places to the left):*

13.55% ÷ 100 = .1355

Step 3. *Multiply total grams by the number from Step 2:*

9072 g. x .1355 = **1229.3 grams of protein in the entire ration.**

Suggested Reading

National Research Council. *Nutrient Requirements of Horses, Fifth Revised Edition.* Washington, D.C.: National Academy Press, 1989.
> *Although this book is written in a fairly rigorous academic style, it is packed with information about nutrients and nutrition, including feed tables listing the nutrient composition of everything that could conceivable end up in a horse's feed tub.*

Harold F. Hintz, Ph.D. *Horse Nutrition, A Practical Guide.* New York: Prentice Hall Press, 1988.
> *Dr. Hintz offers the horseman a thorough and readable treatise on nutrition for every class of horse. Written in a conversational style, "Horse Nutrition" mixes scholarly advice, helpful comments and historical anecdotes into an enjoyable and informative discussion of a difficult subject.*

GENERAL BIBLIOGRAPHY

J. Warren Evans, Anthony Borton, Harold Hintz, L. Dale Van Vleck. *The Horse.* New York: W.H. Freedman and Company, 1990.

Captain M. Horace Hayes, F.R.C.V.S. *Veterinary Notes for Horse Owners.* New York: Prentice Hall Press, 1987.

Frank B. Morrison. *Feeds and Feeding.* Ithaca, New York: The Morrison Publishing Company, 1950.

William T. Keeton. *Biological Science.* New York: W.W. Norton & Company, 1967.

National Research Council. *Vitamin Tolerance of Animals.* Washington, D.C.: National Academy Press, 1987.

The Blood Horse. *Feeding the Horse.* Lexington, Kentucky: The Blood Horse, 1969.

S.G. Jackson, Ph.D. & J.D. Pagan, Ph.D. *Equine Nutrition: Applying the Science.* Versailles, Kentucky: Kentucky Equine Research, 1992.

Christian de Duve. *A Guided Tour of the Living Cell.* New York: Scientific American Books, 1984.

Association of American Feed Control Officers. *Official Publication: 1994*. Atlanta Georgia: Association of American Feed Control Officers, 1994.

John M. Kingsbury. *Poisonous Plants of the United States and Canada*. Englewood Cliffs, New Jersey: Prentice-Hall, 1964.

David L. Heiserman. *Exploring Chemical Elements and Their Compounds*. Blue Ridge Summit, Pennsylvania: TAB Books (division of McGraw-Hill), 1992.

Tom Ivers. *The Fit Racehorse*. Cincinnati, Ohio: Esprit Racing Team, LTD., 1983

William E. Jones, DVM, Ph.D. *Nutrition for the Equine Athlete*. Wildomar, California: Equine Sportsmedicine News, 1989.

Rex A. Ewing. *Organic Trace Minerals: A Case Where Function Follows Form*. LaSalle, Colorado: John Ewing Company, 1994.

Inger Wegger, F.J. Tagmerker and Johs. Moustgaard. *Ascorbic Acid in Domestic Animals*. Copenhagen, Denmark: The Royal Danish Agricultural Society, 1984.

Colin C. Whitehead. *Biotin in Animal Nutrition*. Basle, Switzerland: F. Hoffmann-La Roche & Co., Ltd., 1988.

BASF. *Vitamin E in Animal Nutrition*. Ludwigshafen: BASF.

J.E. Linden. *The Role of Biotin in Improving the Hoof Condition of Horses*. Basel, Switzerland: F. Hoffmann-La Roche Ltd., 1992.

Thomas W. Pearson, Howard J. Dawson, Homer B. Lackey. *Natural Occurring Levels of Dimethyl Sulfoxide in Selected Fruits, Vegetables, Grains, and Beverages*. Washington, D.C.: American Chemical Society, 1981.

Rex A. Ewing. *Chondroitin Sulfates: A Natural Aid for Battered Joints*. LaSalle, Colorado: John Ewing Company, 1995.